mind changing short stories and metaphors

short stories, metaphors, fantasies and dreams for hypnosis, hypnotherapy and NLP

by John Smale

D1422250

This book is a work of fiction. The names, characters and incidents in this book are the work of the author's imagination. Any resemblance to any persons living or dead or any locations or scenarios are purely coincidental.

Published in September 2008 by emp3books,
Kiln Workshops, Pilcot Road, Crookham Village,
Fleet, Hampshire, GU51 5RY, England

Previously published by Exposure Publishing 2008

ISBN-10: 0-9550736-4-2
ISBN-13: 978-0-9550736-4-9

www.emp3books.com

This book is dedicated to those who that have helped me to find inspiration

CONTENTS

v

INTRODUCTION

When used in NLP and hypnotherapy, metaphors have long given insights into the difficulties of people and have shown the ways in which we can escape or improve. If the stories strike a chord with you, then they also show a way out.

These short stories, metaphors and interactive scripts will help you to eliminate negative thoughts and achieve your dreams by allowing you to relax while reading stories that can bring about positive change.

Some of the stories will relax you, others will make you think. Some allow you to enter a light feeling of hypnosis.

Hypnotherapy and hypnosis have been major users of metaphors to show different approaches to problems and their resolution. Milton Erickson, the grandfather of modern hypnotherapy used metaphors to great effect in resolving problems with his patients.

Self hypnosis allows you to enter the areas of your mind where you can become imaginative and optimistic. You can create your dreams and the ways in which you will achieve them.

The most perfect thing about humans is our lack of perfection. It is what drives us to seek improvement. We should always strive to be better, happier, healthier and fulfilled by loving ourselves, our neighbours and life of all sorts on our planet.

When we dream we transport our minds to places where life is better and where your goals should be placed. Positive thoughts eliminate the nightmares we find in sleep and our waking lives.

My dream is to help you to achieve what you want and deserve. Please enjoy this escape to your new reality.

THE BURDEN

A story that shows that when we are overburdened, stressed or abused, we have to break away from the situation to find our true place in life, ideally without violence.

As the dappled stallion grew older, it felt stronger; but as the horse grew older, it felt more and more burdened. And as it became tougher, so the loads in its panniers became heavier so that more rocks and stones could be carried to the top of the hill.

Once there, he was made to squat so that the panniers slid off his back to the ground. This hurt his muscles and legs very much. His legs were always bruised and sore.

This castle was taking an eternity to build and the horse knew that it would be completed after his own lifetime that was becoming shorter and shorter by the day.

The grass was greener on the other hills that he could see from his elevated vantage point that was higher, but this place was barren from the dust that always rained down.

Here his food was dry and coarse, apart from the few pieces of grass that grew by the side of the winding track that he had to plod upwards, day after day after day, on his way to the summit. However, he never got very much of this fresher food before being whipped into taking more steps. Even pretending to be lame, his short breaks became merely brief moments of time before he was hit again.

His hooves were sore from the constant grinding of the sharp gravel on the path, and often little trails of blood would mark where he had limped under the huge weight he had to carry.

On the way back down the hill, the horse had to bear the massive weight of the man who had whipped him to climb up it a little while before.

The horse had been currency in settling a gambling debt with its breeder. That man had raced horses for many years but had lost so much money in his impotent attempts to become rich. Ironically, had he not lost so much, he would have been a wealthy man. His spur to win the pot that was 'so big that he could buy his happiness' was the very thing that drove him to misery.

It was the same feeling that the horse now endured from the lash of his handler; pain in being driven to climb faster with an ever increasing burden with no return of satisfaction or achievement.

One day the panniers were so overloaded that the horse stumbled as he climbed. Nearing the top, the horse was frightened by one of the stonemasons who was ranting and raving at the slowness of the delivery of the rocks. He wanted the bonus he had been promised if he built faster.

Blaming the horse, because there was no other target, he ran at it brandishing his hammer. The horse reared into the air, kicking out with its front hooves. The mason's head was split in two.

Aware of the consequences, the horse reared and kicked harder at the air. The panniers slid off, their contents crushing the cruel handler. All that showed beneath the pile of rocks was a hand holding a whip.

Unencumbered but scared, the horse bolted. He ran down the track, jumped the fence and headed for the green hills. Driven by fear he kept running for a day and a night before he collapsed from exhaustion.

When he awoke he was aware of other horses looking at him. He got to his feet and stared back.

'Who are you?' one of the horses asked.

'I am a pack-horse who has escaped after murdering two men.' He replied.

'But you are a racing horse. You are built for speed rather than for bearing loads. Are you the creature that we have seen on the hill with the new castle?'

'That is me. That was my job and I did it as well as I was able despite the man with the whip.'

The other horses nodded sympathetically.

'Who are all of you?' He asked.

'We are free spirits. We run. We eat the fresh and lush grass. We enjoy being horses rather than the tools and instruments of others. Would you like to join us?'

'Yes, I would, but who carries the whip here. What do I have to do?'

'You have to do but one thing. Understand that your life is about recognising what you are. You are a race-horse who should run your own race. You have been a beast of burden. A beautiful creature that was abused and treated cruelly. Today your true life begins. The loads you carried have been taken from you. The past has gone into the past. The future is what is front of you. You left your burden in that cruel place where you were trapped. Now, at last you are free.'

THE BLACK PIT

Depression often goes with being stuck in the poor circumstances that arise when hope evaporates. The important thing to do is to look into the future. See yourself in a better situation; imagine new people in your life. The old saying goes 'be careful what you wish for.' When you live in gloom the light never goes on because you expect the darkness. Do something positive. Turn the light on and bathe in the radiance of optimism. Wish for a happy future. Those bad feelings pass. Depression is a state of mind. We can change that state when we wish for a better future. That has to be our dream that then becomes a reality.

In the darkest despair of depression, the man had the same feeling as if he had fallen from the cliff that faced a narrow ravine.

He fell deeper and deeper into the darkness of the pit. He imagined jagged black rocks at the bottom that would rip his body into many pieces. He was comfortable with that because his misery would end, but somewhere in his heart he wanted a better outcome.

He had closed his eyes at first but he wanted to know when his despair would be saved by his body smashing into the big boulders that awaited him. He was falling more slowly than he thought he should be. Even this fate was full of slowness and waiting for something to happen.

He opened his eyes to see the fate that awaited him. What he saw was the biggest, bounciest trampoline that there has ever been. It was bright and decorated with pictures of flowers, birds and butterflies. He hit it feet first and the speed at which he fell slowed.

And then stopped.

He was amazed that he was still alive.

Then he started to accelerate upwards and onwards. At first it felt slow and then the pace at which he was being delivered increased until he landed gently on the other side of the canyon. He looked around, astonished by what had happened.

It took him a while to come to a realisation of his situation. There in front of him he could see flowers and butterflies that reflected the patterns on the trampoline.

He could see fields of green grass. He could see pathways that took him into this wonderful place that was light and airy. He could see the friends that he would make in the future.

He looked back to the side of the valley from which he had come. He saw the gloom, the waste, the barrenness, the loneliness that he had experienced. It looked like a dark treacherous desert full of malevolent cacti and poisonous snakes. They swayed as if tempting him to return so that they could hurt him even more.

Every one of his bad experiences seemed to be represented by a part of that landscape that was menacing. Sharp rocks, boggy marshes and debris as if delivered from Hell's waste disposal system.

He turned to face the brighter side. It was if he had travelled from one extreme to the other. Here the landscape was full of beautiful things, every part of this place offered happy and joyful experiences yet to come. Here there were people who were full of delight, full of optimism. The scent in the air had changed from that of rot to that of sweet perfume.

He approached one person who looked friendly, but they all did, and asked if his death had brought him to Heaven.

'No. you are not dead, but now you are alive. You are in the place where we should all live. It is the world as it is without the misery of depression. Without the darkness of pessimism and lack of hope and ambition. This is the real world. What happened to you is that you fell onto a allegorical trampoline that propelled you to a brighter future. It made you aware that life has more to offer than despair.

There is an easier way, however. There is a bridge that spans the canyon. It is made from hope and the desire to look at the future successes of yourself rather than living in the gloom of your supposed failures. It crosses the deep and dark chasm without risk. It is called the Bridge of Positive Thinking. It takes you from a dark state of mind to a bright outlook where happiness is the norm rather than a forlorn dream.'
The man lifted his head and started to plan his life. He thought about what he wanted to do that would make him happy.

He turned his back on the gloomy side of existence and started to walk into the bright side of his life.

Soon he was joined by people who shared his hopes and dreams for a better future, his new friends.

He changed his thoughts from those of self-pity to those of self-worth.

NOTE. Of course, there is only a metaphorical trampoline at the bottom of a cliff. Never take the risk of jumping, use the bridge to cross the darkness instead.

THE PROFITEER

Greed often changes a person into something that is highly undesirable. When men go in the search of profit at the expense of others, they can find that the tragedy of others can hit back.

The restaurant was full of opulence. Oak and leather combined to create the feel of an old palace. The chairs melted around their occupants as they reached for the solid silver cutlery. Aromas filled the air giving hints of the rich food on the menu.

It was staffed by trained and knowledgeable waiters smartly dressed as if they had come from a painting of Paris in the 1920s, rather than smug cheap labour who looked like students enhancing their incomes in other, less grand, places.

The restaurant manager wore a traditional black wrap that came up to his armpits and went down to his shiny shoes. He had a little clipped moustache and a polite smile.

The chefs were trained experts in their craft and who could smell a truffle in a field as well as a pig instead of fast food cooks who could replicate recipes from celebrity cookbooks. The chefs had as many stars between them as a night sky in the summer.

The wealthy man walked in wearing a perfectly tailored, and very expensive, suit. He sat down with his stockbroker to commence a grand lunch. He enjoyed his sumptuous feasts. He wanted to emulate Henry VIII. Food, drink, women and power should have been his motto. In this place even the tossing of bones over the shoulder would have been tolerated openly, but resented in the kitchen.

The man's corpulence was well hidden by his jacket that flopped open as he began to speak.

'Look, I'm not the sort of man who makes money from the simple tragedies of life. I chase natural disasters like earthquakes and floods, the things that folk call Acts of God. Well if God causes them, somebody has to clean up, and that's what I do. I clean up. And that's how I make piles of money, but not very many friends.' He laughed loudly and wiped the resultant dribble from his mouth with his silk handkerchief.

'You see, disaster is always double-sided. If somebody loses, then I make sure I win. Companies don't want to pay out compensation, so they hire me to beat off claims. I work out to be slightly cheaper for them. Then there are the rebuilding contracts. Every time there is a flood or earthquake, my bank manager wants to buy me lunch. 9/11 made me enough to buy a Caribbean island. The tsunami gave me enough to build a mansion on it. Other disasters brought in enough to buy a private jet. You could say that the money floods in and that makes the ground shake for me. My life is perfect when it is bad for others. '

He had emphasised the words 'floods' and 'ground shake' to turn his words into his attempt at humour.

He laughed at his own jokes as the stockbroker nodded his head to hide his embarrassment.

The man continued. 'Global warming is the greatest opportunity that I have found in many years. Houses need flood defences and air conditioning. How is that for a chance to make some more cash? Tragedy tourism must be a good market for those people who give money to disaster funds and want to see where their money has been spent? How about disaster theme parks where paying visitors can experience calamity without risk? Earthquake chambers, dying polar bears in cages, starving people who beg for a little of the visitors' popcorn.'

The stockbroker watched the man wipe a little more dribble from his mouth before starting on his third glass of Château Margaux to wash down his Chateaubriand steak, fresh asparagus and truffle sauce.

He was silent as the greedy man was about to start another tirade of bragging and boasting whilst finishing his cheese.

'No shortage of food or drink in this restaurant, thank God! And it's all paid for by death. By the way, I'll pick up the tab, for the first time.' He laughed as he handed a fat wad of paper money to a nearby waiter.

After he had gestured the waiter and the change away, the man gripped his chest, grimaced and fell off his leather dining chair to the ground, knocking his fine crystal glass off the table to smash in pieces on the marble floor.
The earthquake inside his chest stopped his heart from beating, yet oddly, there were no floods of tears from just the three people who attended his funeral.

His bank manager was sad, however, but the stockbroker was relieved that this person had now lost everything to his own natural disaster and that his death duties might help to build a better world for those who needed it.

'I guess he did pick up the tab, after all...And yes, it was paid for by death.' He thought to himself.

QUICKSAND

Life can present precarious options. The way to be safe is to avoid the pitfalls that can be offered as pleasures such as bad relationships, drugs or jobs without prospects. Be confident enough to make the right decisions. Take those chances that offer benefit and steer clear of those that offer jeopardy.

The woman was stuck in quicksand in the middle of a forest. The more she struggled to get out, the more she sank. This bog was different to the usual mix of sand and water, it was made from swampy emotion, dank and rank.

She fell into the quagmire when she split from her boyfriend. He had used and abused her for years and when she finally had enough, she became brave for a moment and told him.

He told her she was ugly, fat and useless in bed. He had told her that so many times before and she started to believe that it was true.

And then, after smacking her, he left her to live with somebody else that he could exploit, use and abuse.

She sank into gloom. She immersed herself in thoughts of regret. She had no future and was half happy that she was stuck and half miserable that her life could not progress.

A giant was walking along the same path and he saw the woman in the quicksand. He was unable to get close enough to save her because he was so heavy that he would sink in himself. He stood back and unravelled a rope from his backpack. He threw it to the woman who grabbed it.

The giant pulled and pulled and pulled until the woman was freed and was able to stand on solid ground.

She was grateful and thanked the giant.

'Who are you?' She asked.

The giant replied with a voice as deep as thunder. 'I am your future. When somebody is stuck, they have to be aware that the future is what pulls them out of the sticky situation that they are in. Now that you are on the outside of the mire, you are standing on higher ground and you can look for safer paths to walk than the one you were on. When you are stuck in a deep quicksand you can only see the mess that you are in. When you stand tall you can see the options that you have in your life. Your boyfriend was the bait that enticed you into the mud. Now you are free from him, rejoice. He will be the quicksand for other souls that I will have to rescue.'

With that speech over, the giant very carefully walked to a big tree at the edge of the forest and tied the rope around its trunk. He then threw the rope back to the woman.

'Use this rope to make to your journey safe. At the end of this rope is where your future starts. Look into the open space beyond the forest, visualise your happy future and let it unfold for you.'

The woman replied, 'But I have no future. I am ugly,

fat and not good in bed. My ex-boyfriend told me so.'

The giant looked into her eyes as if seeing her soul. 'You are none of those things. Some men feel that they can only keep the beautiful things they have by hiding them in a cage of insults. Be as free of that cage as you are of the quicksand. The things he said are not true. He was projecting his own insecurities onto you. Get on with your life. Enjoy it. You have everything that you need to succeed now that you are free.'

The giant moved on and disappeared from view.

The woman wiped the mess from her clothes and started to hold her head high. She could see the many directions in which she could travel onwards, some safe, some dangerous. She followed the rope to the tree. She stood and looked at the meadows in front of her, smiled and started walking.

She now knew that the best way to avoid traps was to foresee the dangers at the start of a journey rather than to get fixed in a dangerous situation.

The giant might not appear the next time!

THE SWING

Sometimes we need to encourage others to take responsibility for their own achievements through their own efforts. Sometimes helping too much turns to hurt the giver. Be self-assured. Do what you are able to do to help others but without damaging yourself.

'Daddy, push me higher.' The young child was demanding rather than asking as he sat on the seat of the swing in the garden. His father responded by pushing gently on his son's back. He loved his child so much and had promised that he would do anything, and sacrifice everything to ensure his son's happiness.

'Harder. I want to go higher and higher. Come on. Do it for me.'

The man pushed harder and harder until his son had gone as high as was possible. The father had to sit down and rest. He had spent all his energy.

'Dad, I want to go to the best school that I can.'

'But son, I cannot afford it!'

'Then work harder and longer so that I can go.'

So the father worked harder and longer until he could just about afford to send his son to the best school, although he had to arrange loans to pay all that was needed. At the end of each day he would have to sit down and rest.

When his wife left him for another man who wanted

to spend his time and conversation with her, he was sad but knew he had to get used to a different way of living.

'Father, I need to go to the best University that there is. It will cost you a lot but I need clothes that will make sure I fit in with the rest. I will need to join clubs and go to the theatre with my new friends.'

'But son, I cannot afford it! I am already working as hard and as long as I can'

'Then sell the house to raise the money.'

The house was put on the market and the man raised enough money to finance his son's education even though he could only afford to live in a small rented room where, every evening after working as long and as hard as he could, he had to just sit and rest.

When his son graduated, the father thought he could, at last, take things easier but his son needed more clothes for his new job and a sports car to impress the girls in his life.

The father had to keep on working long and hard hours.

At last his son bought a house. It was the house where he had grown up. The swing was still in the garden, although it was rusty and old looking. The son got rid of it.

Then, when he married the woman who made him happiest at the time, the strain was taken from his father after he had paid for half his son's wedding. He had married into a wealthy family that had to have the best for their daughter and that required a contribution from their daughter's father-in-law.

His wife became pregnant and during the birth when the doctor told her to push harder, her husband shouted that she should do better than she was.

'Push harder for goodness sake.' He knew that if he demanded this from his wife, she would respond. After all that was her job and he knew that she loved him. After a long and painful birth his wife gave him his son to hold.

The new mother asked, 'Have you told your father that he is a granddad?'

'Why should I? What interest has he ever shown?' was the reply.

His son grew to be healthy and strong. One day in the garden on the swing his grandfather had bought him, the boy called out.

'Daddy, push me higher.' The young child was demanding rather than asking as he sat on the seat of the swing in the garden.

'No. You do it. Stop being so lazy. How do you think you can get anywhere in life if you never do anything for yourself? I had to do everything for myself when I was growing up. Nobody did anything for me.'

His son moved his legs and arms to swing higher as his father sat and watched.

He was too busy planning how he could get his father-in-law to pay for this child's education and future.

He remembered his own childhood and wondered why his own father had died so young and had left so little behind. 'He was always selfish. I do not think he ever loved me as much as I love my own son.' He thought.

THE MAGIC CARPET

The fear of flying is very often the result of negative associations with emotional turmoil rather than with a flight.

Jill was petrified. Her husband, Jim, had just announced that he had bought tickets for a holiday in Crete, the Greek island in the Mediterranean.

She had not flown since she was a young woman when she went on holiday to Ibiza with her boyfriend at the time. They had spent ten days visiting different nightclubs. It had been a dream beforehand but a nightmare when her boyfriend, who she thought she loved, enjoyed dancing with the other girls that he met in the clubs. Jill had to watch while her man strutted around in a pale imitation of John Travolta.

Pete was like a different person. The relationship was unstable. They started to argue. The holiday with the man she loved was becoming a frightening ordeal.

On their last night Jill decided that they would go to a restaurant instead of a club. Pete was unhappy because he wanted to dance. He drank wine and then brandy and when they returned to their hotel he was drunk.

He drank some more brandy in the bar before they went to bed.

'Arr you joying the 'olidayyy?' He slurred. 'Cos I'm not. I need more sex.'
Jill said, 'Is that why you are dancing with every

woman that you meet. You want to extend your collection of girls that you have bedded.'

He exploded. He hit her on her face and dragged her over to his side of the bed. It was not making love, it was not sex, but more like a rape. Jill wanted to go home.

On the return flight they hardly spoke. Jill gripped the arms of her seat and every noise that she heard was like the sound of her world going down with a bang. When the drinks trolley was unhitched in the galley, she thought it was a wing dropping off because her anguish was at its height. She worried that Pete would drink too much on this three and a half hour escape from his behaviour.

Shortly after their return to England, the affair became stormy. It bumped along for a few days and then it crashed.

A few years later Jill met Jim, a kind and caring man who she started to love from the moment they first spoke. He was a man who drank little but gave all of his attention to this lady he loved so much.

When they married, the honeymoon was in England. Jill did not want to fly and used the excuse of putting the cost of the honeymoon towards their first house.

So, when a few years later, Jim announced his gift, Jill felt panicky and sick inside.

She sought help. This involved telling somebody all about her holiday with Pete. She could not blame him too much, although what he did was unforgivable.

They had been in love and they were both young. She could not blame Ibiza, it had always been there and the clubbing scene was part of the young person's culture. She had to sublimate her fear of Pete and holidays abroad onto something and what better than the aircraft? After all it had taken her to her sad fate.

She cried and cried when she related the story of the times in the clubs when she lost the attention of the man she loved. She cried more at the memory of being hit and raped. She feared that the evil aircraft that Jim had booked would take her to a similar end. And Crete is an island in the Mediterranean as well and she did love her man.

The similarities abounded. Her mind expanded them to the point where she and Pete had fought and split, and projected it onto her relationship with her husband

When this was pointed out by the therapist, she wondered how this revelation would help her. She was still petrified of flying!

New associations were made to push away the negative ones that had been planted by her bad experience.

She imagined a big smile on the front of the plane. She was taught how to breathe in an open way, using her diaphragm rather than her chest. She was shown how to open her knees to reduce tension. She was told to open her arms as if slouching in the aircraft seat.

Then she was asked if she liked fast cars and then to imagine Jim driving a sports car feeling the acceleration as she was eased back into her seat on their way to a perfect restaurant.

When she was a child she enjoyed it when her father drove the family car over the brow of a humped-back bridge, the feeling in the stomach that made her plead for him to do it again. That was the feeling she would get on take off.

She was asked to monitor the bumps in her car on her drive home and to compare those feelings that she took for granted with the same feelings that had scared her on the plane. Turbulence can make no comparison. It is far gentler. What a silly word!

And the noises on the aircraft are what they are supposed to be. The wing flaps coming in after take off and then going out for landing make a gentle purring, whirring noise. The same applies to the wheels.

When the drink and food trolleys are unhitched it is wonderful. It is part of the luxury of flying. People smile as they offer you a drink or hand you a prepared meal. That never happens in our regular lives. And there is the chance to watch a film or listen to music without being interrupted by a telephone.
Still doubtful, Jill accepted the fact that she and her husband would fly to Crete.

The day arrived and they drove to the airport, parked

the car and went inside the terminal building (another bad choice of words!) to check in. Jill practised her breathing and felt fairly relaxed.

They went to the departure gate and to her surprise Jill saw the imagined smile on the nose of the plane. She was even more surprised when she smiled back.

They boarded the plane and took their seats. Jim held her hand and comforted her. The plane lumbered along the taxi-ways to the runway. Jill sat calmly with her knees apart and arms to the side as instructed. She breathed into her stomach and awaited the acceleration. She imagined it was Jim driving her in a bright red Ferrari as it sped along. Then they found the hump-back bridge and her stomach fluttered with pleasure as the plane took off.

She had a mental picture of a beautiful swan swimming, then paddling hard with its feet until the moment when the wings swept downwards and the graceful and elegant bird took to the air. It flew smoothly and gently as it climbed and then settled into a steady flight.

Jill stirred a little as one of the flight attendants offered her a drink. She ordered an orange juice. Jim had a coffee.

The pilot announced that there might be some turbulence and Jill sat quietly to await this monstrous typhoon. As the plane bumped, she turned to Jim and said, 'We must fix the driveway at home, it is bumpier than this.'

After eating a meal and watching a film they were nearly there. The plane landed and they disembarked.

The holiday was wonderful. They walked in the hills, sunbathed on the beaches and ate wonderful Greek meals. Jim was happy to be with Jill and paid her so much attention. He checked she was wearing sun cream and treated her as the lady that she is.

One day Jill bought a postcard to send to the therapist as promised. It was full of good news and even contained the line...'the only problem with the return journey is that it will come too soon.'

The return journey was smooth and steady. She chatted to Jim about the next place that they would visit.

She used to worry about flying, but now she was an old hand at it.

NOTE. For more information about dealing with flying phobias and breathing techniques, see "The Secret Language of Hypnotherapy" by John Smale.

THE BONFIRE

Memories may be attached to objects but never contained by them in such a way that they are destroyed if the object is lost. Reminiscences are held by our minds instead. We never throw those away unless we want, and need, to.

The chair had been an important part of the family's life for a long time. It was now looking a little old and shabby. The decision was taken to throw it out and to replace it with something newer.

In order to dispose of the old chair, the family built a bonfire in the garden.

The flames grew bigger as the paper, and then the twigs, started to burn. The chair had to be dismantled before it could go on the fire. First the cushion that so many people had sat upon.

Mary had a tear in her eye.

'This is the cushion my mother sat upon before she died. And it is where I sat and fed Kate when she was a baby.'

Kate continued the theme.

'This is where I used to sit on Daddy's lap as well. I used to nurse my dolly until Malcolm cut her hair.' She finished with a tone of sarcasm about her brother.

Malcolm made his contribution.
'This is where I used to dream that I was a pilot and

flew the chair around the world.'

Andrew chipped in.

'This is where I first kissed your mother and later it is where I proposed to her.'

Kate and Malcolm groaned their embarrassment.

'Why are we throwing the chair away? Why are we burning our memories?' Mary was almost pleading for a reprieve.

'Simply because it is old and very uncomfortable.' Andrew was firm in his reply as he threw the cushion onto the fire. It burst into flames and disappeared before their eyes.

Andrew then snapped off one of the legs and threw it on. It crackled as the dry wood hit the heat. The same happened with the other three legs.

Mary was a little distraught. 'We are burning our memories so that we can replace them a new chair? It is unfair.'

The children shuddered a little as a loud bang signalled that the wood was burning well.

Andrew had to have his say. 'The chair was ancient. We want a new reclining chair and we did not have the room for it unless we got rid of this rickety old thing.'
He collected the remainders of the chair, told everybody to get back and threw them onto the fire.

The flames shot into the sky as if the chair was praying to the Heavens with its shimmering fingers. It was like the last moments of Joan of Arc.

The next morning, all that was left was the ash of the chair and the wood used to build the fire.

By the next Saturday the trauma of that day was forgotten after the new chair had been delivered and set up.

Kate was sitting in it when her boyfriend visited. 'Wow! Can I sit there?' He asked.

'Only if you give me a kiss first.' She smiled

'Kate. I need to ask you something.' He was looking serious. He kneeled and looked into her eyes. 'Will you marry me?'

Kate pretended to think about the question and replied, 'Of course I will.'

She and her fiancé ran to the kitchen to tell Mary.

Malcolm wondered what the rush was as he sat in the chair for the first time, reclined it and flew his jet fighter into battle. Even at twenty three he had the urge to escape from the reality of life now and then.

Andrew wondered what all the excitement was for when he came in from the garden.

'Daddy, Tom has asked me to marry him and I said yes.' She threw her arms around her father and kissed his cheek. Then she hugged Tom.

'He proposed to me when I was sitting in the chair.' She paused. 'The new chair, that is.'

Andrew smiled. 'So is that where you will suckle your babies?'

Kate feigned embarrassment as she visualised that event happening.

'And is that where I will sit before I die?' Mary burst into squeals of laughter.

Malcolm, by this time was caught by the mood and jumped in. 'And one day I will have to burn it, I suppose!'

Everybody laughed.

The chair seemed to have brought its own luck with it. The old chair had passed its role to a younger player.

It had gone as an item of furniture, but it had passed its own memories across.

BREATH

The Latin word for breath is the same as the word for Spirit, as is the Hindi word 'prana' and the Chinese word 'chi'. Perhaps we have known the connection between breathing and calmness and a peaceful soul a very long time but have failed to recognise the clues!

The Great Architect designed the Earth and made it to perfection.

Everything that was necessary for its development and growth was added, except one thing. The creator gently blew over it and looked on.

The day that Breath was given a home, it uttered a sigh of relief. It had looked for somewhere to live for a long time. Now it saw a place that looked as if it needed inspiration. It chose that dead, barren lump of rock just floating in space. Breath headed for it and landed.

Breath is a strange thing for us to understand. It is able to exist in tiny voids and, also to fill huge expanses. It is an infinity of forms.

Above all else, it had been made to be curious and restless. It became bored easily.

As Breath was infinite it could split into different gases which joined together to form water. The water covered a lot of the planet. This made it more interesting but not for long.
Breath made the water wash bits of the rock into the oceans. The water was mixed with minerals and

salts. When all was ready, Breathe dived into the ocean and entered the mud and mixed with it. Life was begun.

Breath continued to grow life in all shapes and sizes over the years. It lived in the forests and jungles where it made more breath for the planet.

It lived in the animals that grew on the planet, and the animals became as diverse as the plants.

One of the animals was man and he lived a modest life until one day he discovered the warmth of fire. He could burn some of the plants to keep him warm and to cook his food. Fire, like the plants and animals needed Breath as well.

After a long time, mankind found he could use more and more of the plants, animals and minerals to make his life easier although sometimes men would fight to get more of those resources from other men.

And so it went on until Breath started to be stifled by the smoke and fumes from men making more and more comforts for themselves. Its coughing made gales and hurricanes. Breath was being used, perhaps abused, and it was thinking very hard about leaving this planet to find somewhere else where it would be appreciated. After all that Breath had created, mankind was now destroying its endeavours.

The other animals were dying, plants were suffocated and denied water and the minerals were being used up to add to what was called luxury, and to make weapons that would hasten the death of all life.

This became the real definition of what was named civilisation because this also caused misery to the poorer people on the planet. Only a small proportion of humans could live in comfort.

As a result of all that was happening, Breath devised a plan. It would leave the planet and let it return to a lump of rock, barren and wasted.

Then it would return and start all over again but, this time, with the absence of mankind.

SEWER RATS

Compare the lungs and blood vessels with sewer systems and the dirty things that live there. Clean air and water help to prevent the bad things that thrive on filth like tobacco smoke and fat.

Sewer rats sometimes look like something else but their aim is always the same. They want to live in places where they can build nests and expand their families. They are never liked because they can be dangerous, threatening and destructive. They dribble filth, spread disease and they consume anything they can find.

In the sewers of cities and towns, we know where they are, but we are unable to eradicate them fully. We can trap them, we can poison them, but they survive because we keep putting detritus into the sewer system. Without us adding mess they would go away and eventually die.

Well, so much for sewers and the vermin that live in them.

Our bodies are systems that rely on pipes, valves and clean air and water. When we eat we fill the main pipe from our mouth to our backsides with what starts as food and ends its days as sewage. What we do is extract the goodness from the food but we also extract any badness. Sugar and fat are absorbed into the small tubes and clog them, making our hearts beat harder to keep the circulation going.

Of course the heart is a series of tubes. The chambers and valves have to work harder and harder as a result of the waste products in our narrower pipes. Those things that now form platelets of cholesterol.

And cigarette smoke is even better at narrowing our blood vessels because they make them even smaller and smaller.

Imagine that the sewer rats have become so numerous that sewage cannot move through the pipes. And imagine that they live in the aeration system and grow and grow and grow. That is what happens in the lungs although there they are called emphysema, bronchitis and cancer.

We have the choice to prevent those rats in our bodies. We can stop feeding them with smoke filled with tar. We can choose to stop eating so much fat.

We can decide that we need to keep our internal pipes flushed with fresh water and nutrients rather than clog them with fat. We can exercise to help the blood flow through our pipes.

Sewer rats sometimes look like something else but their aim is always the same. They want to live in places where they can build nests and expand their families. They are never liked because they can be dangerous, threatening and destructive. They dribble filth, spread disease and they consume anything they can find.

TAMING THE WILD RIVER

This story is a fairly lightly disguised metaphor about IBS. Relaxation and visualisation are major tools in coping with it. The comparison made is between a violent river flowing to an explosive end and a more peaceful flow that is controlled and less physically disruptive.

A quick note. *If you have IBS, please make your doctor the first point of call just to ensure that it has no physical origin.*

The river stormed its way over the waterfall into the deep plunge pool at its base. The rocks in this pool collided with each other causing abrasion and erosion. The boulders banged into others as if they were balls being shaken in a bag.

Then the water escaped through a small gorge and continued downstream. Later in its flow, loggers threw tree trunks into the river where they knocked together and battered the banks as they travelled around the bends.

They crashed, smashed and thudded their way along for miles and miles. It was like having big pieces of food caught in the U-bend of a kitchen sink. The waters were very muddy.

Every so often, the logs would cause stoppages as they hit the rocks in the river. Sometimes they were like wild bulls charging along totally out of control. This was a destructive stampede that was busting a gut to get to its destination.

The situation was unbearable to the land, the river banks and the wildlife that lived nearby.

When the logs eventually reached the mouth of the river, they pressed against the lock gates until, with no warning, they shot out into the sea as an uncontrolled mass.

What was needed was a way to slow everything down.

Methods were sometimes used to reduce the speed of the water. Temporary dams were built but they would be eroded after a while and things returned to the way they had been before. Very little seemed to help to assuage the agony and hurt being caused. This temporary relief was often the only thing that offered help.

Then, as if by magic, the waterfall and the river changed. It was as if relaxation and the release of all those stressful things came into the picture.

Now the waterfall had a gentle start as it eased its way down the hillside into a beautifully sculpted basin that swallowed the flow until the water was ready to move on.

As this river trickled along, bits of soft earth were dissolved into it and the smooth mixture was able to gently move around the bends without bumping or knocking anything.
It was an easy movement and passed along its way with nothing more than an occasional gurgle. The river banks absorbed this different situation and assimilated the change.

No more logs were thrown into the river. There was no more banging against the banks, no more log jams as it eased on its way.

Before this metamorphosis, the banks of the river seemed to squeeze the water and chunks of wood as if trying to get rid of them. These spasms were uncomfortable and made the land shudder with distaste.

Now the bits of the land that it had transported were deposited softly onto the banks of this river. Now the surrounding countryside could digest the sustenance given by the stream.

The water was now placid and calm. Its soothing movement was like a kind massage as it eased its way along. No more rush, no more uncontrolled flare-ups. Now it was just a balmy and pacifying natural motion to the end point of the process.

One major shift had been that the lock gates had been changed. Beforehand, they had opened into the ocean rather than the river so that when pressure built up, they would unexpectedly release the mass of water and debris of their own accord.

Now they faced upstream so that they could only open when the lock-keeper decided. There would be no more unexpected floods, no more tidal waves.

Therefore, when the river reached the point where it would empty itself into the ocean, it felt cleaner.

Rather than being violently expelled into the sea as it was before, it now passed its way out in a controlled way.

What had once been a distressing torrent through the narrow passages of the valley was, now, an easy, controlled and calm journey to its closing stages.

As a footnote, when you compare a picture of the stomach and the tubes leading in and out it is surprising how much it looks like a waterfall and the shape of the pool that is eroded.

THE CORPORATE WIFE

When people devote too much time to making careers and money, they can lose the more valuable things in their lives. When the axe finally falls, those people can return to a home full of strangers.

The man had a strikingly beautiful mistress but she was very demanding. She wanted his time, his energy and his devotion.

He also had a wife. She was also demanding of his time, love and devotion. He found it difficult to share what little time he had between them.

Whenever he saw his mistress, he felt guilty. He felt that he was cheating on his wife. Yet, when he was with his wife he felt that he was cheating on his mistress.

He knew older men who had been in the same situation. Some had forsaken their mistresses. Others had left their wives to spend more and more time with their mistresses. However, these men had lost a lot of money or peace in the process.

This man knew that his mistress kept him happy. She cared for him. When he was with her he felt alive.

When he was with his wife he felt stressed and pressurised. She expected his full attention. He had so little time to spend with himself. Sometimes, he just wanted to sit to think. Then his wife called him lazy and uncommitted. All he wanted to do was to make her happy. In order to do this he had to work harder and harder. He wanted time to think of new ways to keep her content, to keep the relationship going.

One day his mistress asked him to leave his wife and go to live in the country, far from the pressure. The man was nervous. This would be such a change to his life and he was still reliant on his wife for so many things.

The following day fate stepped in. His wife called him for a meeting. He was told in no uncertain terms that he had become inadequate and he was told to leave for ever. He was even given some money by his wife in the settlement to tide him over for a while.

He protested that he was only 50 years old and he had given his wife beautiful progeny and had nurtured them while they grew. Now they would be given to somebody else to look after.

This plea fell on deaf ears. He was asked for his keys and was told to leave immediately.

When he got home, his mistress was sympathetic. She loved this man passionately, even though he had spent so much time away from her.

'Look. The children have grown up and have left home now. At last we have the time that we needed to rebuild our lives together. Throughout our marriage I have always felt like your mistress rather than your wife. You seemed to be married to your company rather than me. I was always jealous of the time you spent working and the demands that were made on you. Now can I stop feeling like your mistress and start again as the wife that I am, and have always been?'

It took time for the man to get to know his real wife again and to learn about his two children. He forgot about the products he had launched while working, his progeny as they were referred to.

At last, he discovered that life offers more than stress. He moved to the country with his real wife and enjoyed the rest of his days. She was no longer the mistress that he could only see when the company he was married to would let him.

His corporate wife continued in her own sweet way. She remarried time and time again. She would suck the talent and blood from those young enthusiastic and willing suitors and then throw them away like a cross between a Gorgon and a black widow spider.

THE TWO FIRES

Everybody has quarrels from time to time. They are about reaching warm understanding as two opinions are moulded into an agreement. However, when quarrels turn to angry rows, the outcome can be so destructive that lives are ruined. The following metaphor represents people's lives as a grand house that is danger of being burnt to the ground unless measures are taken to stop the uncontrolled fires.

The house was a beautiful old building. It had taken many years to build. On the ground floor there was a big entrance hall, a lounge, a dining room, kitchen and study.

Upstairs, there were four bedrooms. One was for the husband and wife, one for their daughter, one for their son and one for friends to stay over.

As it was an old house, each room had a log fireplace which added warmth and character to the high level of decoration.

That sets the scene for a blissful life.

The only problem was that the man and woman had huge problems with their bad tempers. It was if the smallest spark could ignite a furious inferno of bitterness and hatred.

When the fire subsided, the damage remained and the couple painted over the smoke stains and carried on as if nothing had happened.
Every time it got worse. The flames erupted and

there was a huge risk that the house would eventually burn down to the ground. The house represented everything that was precious to the couple. These things were their friends, children and possessions that had taken years to make, love and acquire.

Sometimes the man threw too much into one of the hearths and the flames spewed into the room and licked around the furniture. When his wife added her rubbish to the conflagration then the risk became even greater. Escalation and retribution took the situation to a place that was highly dangerous and destructive.

In a calm moment, the man and his wife agreed that they should install water sprinklers in every room so that if the fires in the fireplaces flared up, then something would automatically extinguish the flames before the blaze took over and took away all that they held dear.

From that moment things got better. They learnt never to overload the fires, never to throw the debris from their pasts onto the heat.

They realised that their relationship was about both of them winning by giving a little rather than a war where only one side wins and the other is beaten into submission and the ultimate loss of everything.

They talked to each other about the issues in their lives and marriage, about their hopes, dreams and ambitions. They became parts of a team along with their children and friends.

After that there were no more embarrassing explosions of anger, no more sparks of resentment and jealousy.

The fire they kindled was from the heat of a solid relationship, from the warmth of love.

They were able to sit back and enjoy the glow from the controlled heat rather than burn to obliteration in the inferno.

THE PROBLEM WITH HEIRLOOMS

When people bring their own problems into the lives of others, then the recipient needs to know how to stop being negatively affected. Just because a parent has had bad experiences, it never means that those things will be replicated. We must live our lives as the main player, not as a support act.

'Janet, when I die I want to leave you something that will remind me of you.' The middle aged lady smiled as she made her promise to her daughter.

As she left the room, the younger woman replied. 'You have given me enough already. I do not need anymore.'

The daughter cried softly as she slumped onto her bed. She had always been a sad person. She only ever saw the bad side of life. Her fate had been sealed from her early childhood. Her mother and father argued, sometimes violently. No matter what she said or did she was unable to stop the constant disagreements.

In her own relationships she had looked for a man who would offer her safety and respect but she was only able to find people who would use her and then send her away.

She acquired the belief that she was worthless and that she would have to spend her life looking after her mother, Frieda. Even those times when she had met a man who seemed as if he could be gentle and kind, her mother would vet him to make sure that he would not turn into her ex-husband, Janet's father.

She would eventually do enough to ensure that the relationship would never flourish beyond the first flush of courtship.

Janet could not hold a job. She had no career other than being a servant to her mother. She had tried to work in a factory packing large boxes with smaller ones but the tedium was too close to the monotony in her home life.

What Janet had inherited from her mother was sadness and despair. She needed nothing more from her while she was alive and certainly nothing when she died and that would be in a great number of years time, probably.

'Look. You should be grateful. I gave you life. I gave you opportunity and I gave you support.' Janet's mother had a wonderful ability to blackmail.

Janet could only think her reply, she was never allowed to express it. 'Then you took my life away for your own comfort. Look at yourself. Fat, lazy and selfish.'

What she actually answered was, 'Yes I know. And I am grateful, mother. I wish I could do more for you.'

Sometimes heirlooms break, or they are broken deliberately.

On Midsummer's Day Janet organised a picnic on the top of a high hill near the house. She packed a basket with sandwiches, fruit and cold drinks. She put them in her car with a blanket and a portable chair for her mother to sit on.

She then helped her mother to get dressed and took her to the car. She sat in the passenger's seat and watched with the eyes of a hawk as Janet drove to Ham Hill.

'Watch that car. Watch that bicycle. Watch that child.'

Every few yards Frieda told her what to do even though she had never driven in her life.

'You know that picnic basket is an heirloom. My mother gave it to me in her will. She was a spiteful old cow. Hated me. Ruined my life. She never warned me about men and if she had then I would never have married your father. That is why I insist on you being more careful than I was. Men are only after one thing. I hate them.'

Only after Janet had set the blanket on the ground, put the sandwiches on the plates, poured the drinks and put up her mother's chair did she go to the car to help her mother out. She led her to her chair. Before she sat down she had even more to say.

'Your grandmother was the worst mother than anybody could have.'

In spite, Frieda attempted to kick the picnic basket as she passed it. She missed, fell backwards and broke her leg.

In agony, Frieda shouted and cursed as Janet used her cell phone to call an ambulance.

When it arrived, Frieda was still shouting at Janet,

even though her daughter had wrapped her in the blanket and had comforted her as much as possible.

'You did that on purpose. I saw you trip me. How can you repay all the love I have given you with such a callous act?'

Peter, the first paramedic to jump from the ambulance, was a handsome man. Frieda's demeanour changed immediately. Frieda was examined, comforted and placed on a stretcher.

Peter suggested that Janet drove to the hospital at a safe speed so that she could be with her mother. The ambulance sped away.

By the time Janet arrived at the car park of the hospital, Frieda was being operated on. It was an emergency. As she walked towards the main entrance, Peter was walking towards her. It was the end of his shift.

He recognised Janet and stopped to tell her that her mother was being operated upon so there was no need to rush. He offered to buy her a coffee in the hospital's café and they walked together.

'Your mother seems a tough old thing. She will be alright, I am sure.' Peter was reassuring Janet.

Janet could not help saying, 'That's a shame. I had a funny feeling that granny was acting from beyond the grave. My mother said some bad things about her and when she went to kick the picnic basket, she fell over.' Then she laughed. 'Oh, I am sorry. I shouldn't laugh, should I?'

Peter laughed as well. 'I take it you two don't get along that well.'

Janet told him her story and how her life had been contained and trained as well as a bonsai tree.

It transpired that both were single and unattached so it was natural that they should start to date when it was convenient to hospital visiting and ambulance shifts.

As Frieda's leg healed, so their relationship blossomed. When Frieda was discharged from hospital, the dilemma became Janet looking after her and building her bond with Peter. Janet became stronger. She would no longer be bullied by that old lady. It made sense that Peter moved in with Janet.

A home help was organised as Janet trained to be a support technician on ambulances so that she could have a career that would keep her close to Peter.

When they got married, Janet's mother asked what she would like as a present. 'How about a family heirloom?'
Janet, now more assertive having achieved so much using her own resources, replied, 'The heirlooms that this family had all need to be burnt and thrown away. Our inheritance should be love rather than bitterness, our future is more important than our past.'

Janet's father gave her away at the wedding. She had made contact with him after meeting Peter.

She perhaps understood, now, why he had been like

he had. There was a lot to discard with him as well. She knew that her marriage would never be like that of her parents. It would be based on two loving people sharing happiness with each other.

A WHALE OF A TIME

Every so often we need to dump our personal, emotional rubbish. We need to take a deep breath and get on with our lives in a clean and fresh way.

The whale swam around its ocean and enjoyed its life. It had its mate and their offspring to give love and companionship. It was a happy whale.

However, in its sweeping up of plankton, it would collect detritus in its mouth. This would build up and inhibit the absorption of its food, making it tired and irritable. As it swam around in the depths it usually loved watching the fishes and corals but as it became more lethargic and depressed the enjoyment became rarer and rarer.

There came a time when the blue and clear water seemed to be dark grey and murky. It felt cold and his mate and children annoyed him just by being around.

One day, a huge whale swam close to him. 'Isn't life wonderful!' it squeaked in that long high whistle that whales communicate with. 'The sea is endless as it goes around the world. Apart from whaling ships, we have nothing o fear.'

Our whale, in a squeaky whine replied. 'There was something good about my life once, but now I can only see, and feel, darkness.'

The big whale told him to follow his wake. They swam to the surface. Then the older and wiser whale told the younger one to expel all the air from his lungs and to take a massive in-breath. Our whale ejected the air in his lungs through his blowhole with such vigour that the noise could be heard for miles. The mist it created made the nearby shipping sound their foghorns.

Then the Godfather of whales told his younger charge to spit out all the debris that had collected in its mouth. With another gigantic breath the rubbish was exorcized.

Feeling so much better, our whale took another breath and dived to rejoin his family.

The bigger whale followed. It said, 'Whenever you feel the way you did, dark and bleak, all you have to do is take a break, take a breath and dump the rubbish you have collected in your life. Litter from the past hurts the present. There is never room for junk in anything.'

Our whale was new again. He played with his children, chatted with his mate and saw the colours of the fish and plants again as bright and wonderful things.

If, in the future, he ever felt that life was bad again, he knew what to do; dump personal emotional rubbish, take a deep breath and get on with life in a clean and fresh way.

THE MEDIUM IS THE MESSAGE

Sometimes too much information can be dangerous. At other times it is good to know where truth should sit.

The old lady walked, hesitantly, into the cold and darkened room. The medium gestured for her to sit down. Silence was important. The lady fiddled with her wedding ring and, with her head down, waited.

She was wearing a smart but unfashionable dress that matched her handbag that was held on her lap. She looked tired and weary.

"I am getting a message from a man who has passed over." The medium started. "He was quite old when he went."

The old lady nodded her agreement.

"He was your husband and he passed quite recently, I think. He is still with you, watching out for you and he misses you very much."

The old lady commented. "Yes, you are right. My husband died four months ago after a short illness. He did not suffer too much and after fifty years of marriage I wanted to know that he is alright."

"Of course he is. He is telling me that everything is fine. He mentioned children, does that mean anything to you?"

"Yes we had two children and they gave us five grandchildren. One of them…"

"I think your husband said that one is with him, now."

"No. They are all still here, on Earth"

"I think he is referring to one that might have been lost as a miscarriage."

"Oh. I don't know about that although my daughter Jeannie went through some problems a number of years ago. That must be it."

There was a long pause during which the medium bobbed her head slowly.

The old lady asked her question. "Can you ask Harry where he left his Will? I know he did one but we can't find it."

"He is very faint, but I think he said look in the safe."

"We never had a safe but we have a special place where we kept all the valuable things like jewellery."

"That might be the place. Is it in the house?"

"Yes it is in the bedroom over the kitchen. Under the floorboards, next to the dressing table."

"He mentioned that. He said to make sure that the house is safe."

"Yes it is. I always lock the house up when I am out for security."

"Good. Some neighbourhoods are more dangerous than others."

"Where we live, I mean where I live, is alright. I have good neighbours and they are always around except on Sunday morning when we all go to Church."

"So where is that?"

"St Peter's."

"No. Which part of town." The medium laughed and the old lady chuckled back. "Very often knowing where somebody lives can help me to ask the spirits for more information about things."

"Oh. I see. I live in number 32, York Street. Not too far from the church. About half a mile."

"Your husband sends his blessing and says to take care of yourself and the children."

The old lady read into the medium's shuffling that it was time to go. She passed a small bundle of paper money over to her and, despite the apparent pushing away of the fee, the medium coyly picked it up.

"God bless you. You know so much." The old lady said.

"More than most people think." Was the reply.
The following Sunday morning, at ten o'clock, the old lady left her house to meet her neighbours to go to the ten thirty service. At ten twenty, a man broke into the house through the back door. He ran upstairs, worked out which bedroom the valuables were hidden in and lifted the carpet to expose the floor. There was a little door cut into the boards which he opened. He put his hand into the space.

As the police came into the room he pulled his hand out so quickly that he nearly broke his wrist..

As they dragged him to the front door, the old lady looked at him and said, "The medium was unable to foresee this. And by the way, my husband will be back soon from his game of golf. Not every old lady is as gullible as your mother thinks."

Just a little while later, a young lady walked, hesitantly, into the darkened room. The medium gestured for her to sit down. Silence was important.

The medium started to cold-read this new visitor for hints and clues as to her problem and her financial status.

The young lady opened her handbag before arresting the medium.

"I can see that your future is in a jail". The policewoman laughed as she put the handcuffs on the fake.

THE FERAL CAT

How things can go wild.

The kitten was loved from the moment that it was bought from the pet shop. It was fed well and grew quickly.

After the novelty of its smallness, it wanted to be loved even more than it was and started to scratch the furniture because when it did, its owners stroked it to offer an alternative to chastisement. This, of course, led to more damage and more attention. Soon the curtains were torn and tattered. Then the bedding, then the goldfish.

The cat was wild. It even hissed and arched its back when its owners came near. The dog was ripped on its nose.

"The cat has gone wild, but I still love it." The woman said.

"We have to do something." Her husband replied.

The cat was netted and taken away by the local charity for the welfare of animals. They released it into the wild where, being unable to hunt as a cat, at first, just enjoyed killing and hurting other creatures.

Eventually it mixed with the native feral cats and at first they enjoyed its company. However the wild life was too much for this cat and it wasted away to the point where it was too weak to defend itself against the natural wild cats that now turned on it. The cat was rescued by a woman who was walking in the woods. She took it home and gave it love, but the cat was helped to adjust to its life by being encouraged when it was good and corrected when it was bad. It gave up its wild ways and just slept in safety and peace through most of its last days.

After the cat had been originally taken away, the woman told her husband that she was pregnant. There was much joy in the house and the man busied himself in repairing all the damage in time for the birth of their child.

The boy was loved from the moment that he was born. He was fed well and grew quickly.

After the novelty of its smallness, and the arrival of his sister, he wanted to be loved even more than he was and started to break his toys because when he did, his parents cuddled him to offer an alternative to chastisement. This, of course, led to more damage and more attention.

When the lad reached his teenage years he started to mix with some other lads who enjoyed experimenting with drink and drugs. They broke windows to rob houses and cars.

When the effects wore off, he took stronger and harder drugs. He stole from his parents to finance his life style.

The overdose that put him on life support in the hospital nearly killed him but he survived. All he wanted at that point was the love of his mother and father and sister. They gave him the help he needed to get off the drugs. They praised him for doing well and corrected him when he was bad.

The damage had been done, however. When their son became paranoid and aggressive his parents had to call for help.

"Our son has gone wild, but I still love him." The woman said.

"We have to do something." Her husband replied.

The young man was taken away by the local authorities. After some treatment they released him into the wild where, being unable to work, he just enjoyed hurting other people.

Eventually he mixed with the local gangs and at first they enjoyed his company. However the wild life was too much for him and he wasted away to the point where he was too weak to defend itself against the gang leaders that now turned on him.

Sadly, nobody was able to rescue him and he took his final overdose on the same day as the cat died.

TALKING TO THE LITTLE GUYS

Our whole system is loyal. It will do whatever we ask it, whether it is beneficial or not. The little loyal guys in our heads are our best friends but can be our worst enemies.

I remember a cartoon from my childhood where inside a man's head there were little men who were the operators of the body. A little man with a telescope looked out of the eye, a big bass drum was the eardrum, cranks and pulleys made things move.

What a wonderful representation of the thought centres of the mind. Imagine that these little guys are totally loyal to you and will do anything you ask without question.

So, if you tell yourself that you dislike something, then never be surprised if these small characters ensure that you will have an experience that will confirm your instruction.

"I panic when I fly." The person thinks.

"What did the boss say?" The little ones ask. "We need to panic when we are flying. Is that right?"

"OK. So we will. Hey we are near a plane. Sweat glands, please make sweat. Adrenalin flow, heart start beating faster. Digestion stop. Emotions switch to 'panic'. Muscles tighten and grip. Breathing get rapid and shallow." And so on and on. We can imagine the alarm claxons going off like in a film about a submarine under attack.

The person gets exactly what he wanted. The little guys are so faithful to their master they never question whether their reaction is beneficial. Like well drilled soldiers they carry out their commands without evaluation, only fidelity.

And they have a failure with communication. They never hear the word 'not'.

"I will *NOT* panic when I fly." Is heard as "I will panic when I fly".

We have to learn a new language that we should use to speak to those little guys in our heads, such as, "When I fly I enjoy the experience. I am calm, confident and in control."

"What did the boss say?" The little ones ask. "We need to enjoy flying. Is that right?"

"Breathing slow down and use the diaphragm. Sweat glands stop producing. Heart slow down to a relaxed beat. Digestion start up and prepare for an in-flight snack. Emotions switch to 'enjoy'. Muscles loosen and relax." And so on and on.

The old expression that we get what we wish for often happens because we assume that something bad will happen and those thought centres in our heads ensure that the outcome is the one wanted.

Positive thinking is about good and accurate communication with our minds. Sports psychology spends a great deal of its effort on visualising success. The athlete runs the race in his/her mind and sees the result they want over and over again.

When that person runs or jumps or throws then the little guys in their minds do their absolute best to achieve that result in reality.

Counter to that, if an athlete sees failure, the outcome is obvious. Their bodies, driven by their minds achieve that goal of failure without question.

In our lives our goals might be something other than athletic. In relationships, visualise peace and harmony free from anger. In our careers see success. In our bodies see health. When the little guys are on our sides and are striving for what we want, the sky is the limit.

NOTE. For more information about the language we need to use and the words we need to avoid, see "The Secret Language of Hypnotherapy" by John Smale.

STABILISERS

Gaining independence and freedom requires calculated risks rather than foolish ones.

Susan, a thirty year old woman, cycled along the path in her garden. One of the stabilisers that kept her bicycle upright hit a stone and she came to a halt. At least she had not fallen off.

Sarah, the three year old girl, cycled along the path in her neighbouring garden. One of the stabilisers caught a stone and she came to a halt. At least she had not fallen off.

The woman heard the girl laughing and looked over the fence. The girl saw her and started talking. "Why do you have lizers on your bike? Daddy says that you are not right. You must be silly."

"Stabilisers, you mean. No, I am not silly but I need them in case I fall off and hurt myself." The woman replied.

The little girl smiled. "My daddy says that mine will be taken off soon and I will ride my bike without them."

"But you might fall off and cut your knee or your hand." The woman replied. "I have lived my whole life without taking any foolish risks whatsoever."

"But Susan, you must have missed so much." The little girl's mother, Mary, had been listening to the conversation. "Had I not trusted my own judgement enough then I would never have met Sarah's father.

She would not have been born. I would still be living with my parents. Jim would never have taken risks at work and he would still be doing a menial job rather than doing what he does, accountancy. Learning to take risks that are within reason is essential to moving on. I know that when Jim takes the stabilisers off Sarah's bike, she will wobble, maybe fall off, maybe get a few bruises. Yet in that way, and with Jim there to stop her from hurting herself too badly, she will learn to ride a bicycle on her own. She will grow up and perhaps ride around the World. Who knows? What I do realise is that she has to take a few risks in order to succeed."

Feeling somewhat like a stern teacher, Mary asked her neighbour if she would like her to help her to learn to ride her bicycle without stabilisers.

Susan thought for a while. "Well, that would be nice but let me think about it. I don't want to hurt myself because I am booked to do a bungee jump next week as part of my company's confidence building course. Another part of it is to ride a bicycle blindfolded to get to grips with the sense of orientation. I was practicing with my eyes closed. If I fell off then all of my employees would have the first laugh. I have always taken calculated risks, never foolish ones that would always be doomed to failure. The risks I take are evaluated and planned so that I never fall off my bicycle, or business project.

You see, I have always been too aware of damaging myself physically or financially to gamble. The odds are stacked against the gambler. Las Vegas always wins. I decided that to succeed I had to become the casino. I make sure that within risk I will always win against the person who is reckless rather than shrewd. My business was built step by planned step. Sure I could have lost everything at any point but as long as I took money from gamblers rather than gave it to them I knew I would profit in the end. The stabilisers on my bike are to ensure that when riding with my eyes closed, if I hit a stone, as I did, I would never harm myself. My confidence building course would be a failure if my best managers hurt themselves and were unable to work for me. I am evaluating their risks"

Mary walked away as Susan asked her if she would like to come along to her team building week. Mary was sure she heard a sarcastic tone in Susan's voice that matched her own when she had first spoken to her neighbour.

STAG MAN

The old stag is always beaten by a younger challenger, sooner or later.

Matthew Stag, the Chief Executive, sat in his office with his feet on his desk. He was tired but he knew that he would have to be at his best when talking to the company that wanted to buy him out.

He preened himself, adjusted his tie and strutted like his animal namesake to the boardroom. He timed his entrance to perfection. The rivals were already seated on one side and his directors on the other. They looked at their boss with admiration and subtle gestures of support. As he was about to speak, a young man stood up and said, "If you don't mind, I have prepared our agenda. The first item is the acquisition of your company and its assets."

"Not if I have my bloody way." The CEO replied, spitting his words rather than delivering them with grace. Look, you don't want to lock horns with me. I have been around a lot longer than you, you young buck."

The well dressed young man stood even taller. "Look you are stuck in a rut and you need fresh blood to put stock into your company. I can bring a new breed in here. Your employees have been used for too long."

The two men fought with much arguing and posing.

They battled long and hard until the CEO announced his resignation and trotted slowly back to his office for the last time. The directors were busy fawning over their new boss. Doe eyed women flirted and the young men recognised the danger in this new situation. They offered loyalty and support openly, knowing that one day they would challenge this new head of the herd.

Matthew returned home, a little drunk, and announced to his wife, "They have put me out to pasture. I am dead meat now. They want to hang me."

He looked at the portrait of him as a younger man. There he was, standing on a hill with the Scottish mountains in the background highlighting his grandeur.

"At least they didn't want to hang my head on the wall."

Diana, his wife, wanted to know what this younger man looked like.

"You as well, my dear!" Matthew bellowed before he went into his garden. Foaming at the mouth, he started attacking his trees.

DRY ICE

Using alcohol and drugs to camouflage and disguise situations never gets rid of memories, they only increase the damage.

There was a television programme once where people would want to imitate their idols. It was called "Stars in Your Eyes". They would appear as they were in normal life, talk about themselves and then disappear into a fog of dry ice to reappear as their hero to the words, "tonight I would like to be..."

They all seemed to be nice people with an ambition to be like somebody they admired. After the show they would have returned to the nice people they started as.

Take a different scenario. Call it "Fools in Other's Eyes". Then give them alcohol or drugs. Let them escape into the fog and appear as drunks or drug addicts. They could act out what seemed to be a better life, free from responsibility and social awareness. They could stagger, mumble and steal.

In their minds, of course, they were suave and sophisticated. They were perfect examples of the human race, but to the audience they were wasters and dangerous people who were out of their heads.

When they sobered up or came down from their high, they would have to return to the lives they had before but, very often they would have to face the damage that had been caused to themselves and to others.

The camouflage wore off. No longer being able to

hide, they could be seen in their full lack of glory.

And where would this programme end? The heat winners could go through to a grand final which would give points in different categories. Extra scores for "Beat the wife", and "Crashing the Car with the Worst Outcome", "Being the Best Role Model to Create Dysfunctional Children" and the favourite, "Wrecking the Brain".

Viewers would tune in every week to watch the chaos. Then, of course there could be a follow up programme, a spin-off. "Where Did The Problems Come From In The First Place?"

The audience could press the buttons on a pad to vote for "Childhood Abuse", "Sibling Rivalry", "Peer Pressure", "Lack of Confidence" and many others.

Drink and/or drug abuse often allows the victim to make an apparent escape into what seems to be a brighter and more interesting place. That is the illusion. In there, there is only more darkness and gloom which becomes apparent when the person sobers up or comes down from a high.

The best way to escape from a grim past is to expose that history to somebody who will listen, understand and help the sufferer to find a clean and sober way forward.

Dry ice can only mask something. The change is an illusion that never lasts.

TICKS ON THE HEAD

Removing the irritating emotional parasites that live on us.

After walking through the emotional jungle that was his life, Eric's head was covered in ticks. They were sucking the life-blood from him, feeding on the distressing debris that had been caused by the simple act of living.

There was one that was large and green even though it was bloated on blood. Eric knew it was called Jealousy. He had started out life jealous of the attention his siblings got from their parents. He hated his brothers and sisters. As this thing grew it fed on his relationships with his friends, his girlfriends and every association that he attempted to develop. It was a monster.

Close to it was another tick that was red and fat. Rather than sucking his blood, this one was stabbing at his head with aggressive vengeance. Eric called it Anger. It has destroyed so much of his life. Combined with Jealousy, he was being drained of any residual happiness that was in him.

There were more of them. Depression, a dark grey one that lived on his left eyelid, keeping any light from reaching him. Then there was Pessimism that lived on his right eyelid and prevented Eric from seeing anything that could be hopeful or beautiful.

Then there was Fear. This prevented him from doing anything that would broaden his horizons. Instead he lived in the darkness that was his restricted life.

There were many others.

At night the ticks seemed to become more active. They nibbled away at his thoughts keeping him awake and causing more problems that were immediately spotted by other ticks that wanted sustenance.

Desperate for relief, Eric tried using alcohol to kill the ticks. He used it internally and externally but the ticks just seemed to stay put, regurgitating saliva, making his head sore and causing more pain. He used hot matches but they only burnt him and caused more pain.

He then got some special tweezers, grasped the ticks, one by one by the head, and pulled. With each one that he extracted he felt slight pain but that was nothing when compared to the subsequent relief he experienced. He dropped each one into a small fire he had set. It was as if each tick was full of the essence of the problem it had been feeding on and with the creatures' removal so emotional disinfectant was applied to help clean and sanitise the pain and anguish that had been there before.

He called the tweezers Optimism and Hope. He used them with a new belief that despite the fact that the emotional parasites had seemed to paralyse his life, he could get rid of them and start to live again.

He contacted his siblings and met them as a grown man. He left his childhood resentments behind. They belonged to a young boy rather than the adult he now was. He started to believe that friends and girlfriends could love him for who he was. He became loving and kind now that his aggression and anger had been removed.

He knew that life was for reaching out to give something that was benevolent rather than for feeding the negative and malevolent emotional parasites that had used and drained him.

THE QUEUE AT THE POST OFFICE.

A little patience saves more than time when getting irritated and storming out, then coming back later when there is no queue.

The man stood behind four other people in a queue at the village Post Office. It was 11.00 o'clock in the morning. An old lady was paying her bills and was taking so much time in doing so. The man became so impatient. After what seemed an eternity, the old lady was done. She slowly packed her paperwork into her bag and left. It was now 11.05.

The man uttered a sigh of relief that became a whispered curse as an old man took out a pile of papers and set them on the counter.

He took a long time to cash his pension and then he started to pay his bills one by one.

Our man mumbled and swore under his breath at this theft of his time. Eventually the old man packed up and left. Now it was 11.09.

It repeated again. This time another old lady piled letters and parcels onto the counter. The man could not hold his temper and blasphemed at the old lady. "Why the Hell do old people need so much time, my time, to sort out a few .simple things?"

He span on his heel and stormed out. At first the other people in the Post Office were shocked, and slowly they all started to laugh.
The impatient man walked around aimlessly for twenty minutes and returned to the Post Office.

There was no queue this time.

He bought some stamps and was pleased that he did not have to wait. Congratulating himself on how much time he had saved, he left the counter at 11.32, twenty minutes after the fourth, and last, member of the queue had gone after buying one stamp.

He complained to the Postmaster about the selfishness of old people and then he went home to relate to his wife how sensible he had been to leave the queue and how much time he had saved by doing so.

Sadly, he never grew old enough to collect his pension to pay his own bills. His high blood pressure finally took its toll.

WHERE'S THE PROPHET IN THAT?

When the prophet returned to Earth He started with a small audience of followers. The new messages that he brought were strong and wise.

They told about how mankind was killing the world that God had set them upon. They told how greed was the greatest sin because it encouraged people to kill off the plants and animals so that the land that belonged to them could be sold off for profit.

They told how the aggression of one country against others in the search for the ownership of the resources of the world would end in misery.

Those carbon based things such as diamonds and oil were placed there at the same time as other carbon based things, mankind included. Imagine diamonds eradicating people with guns. Imagine oil killing the human species with bombs. Well, how about pollution, gas guzzlers and Global warming?

Being the 21st century, this new prophet went to a public relations guru with his message.

"Look, son, although the message is good, the need to spread the message does not meet my criteria for sales. If you become a celebrity then there could be a market."

The prophet was aghast. "What do you want me to do? Go on TV and take part in celebrity games in which the prize is a short lived revival of a career? What we need is for the message to be spread."

"Well, you could write a book, but for it to sell you need to be famous already. The message you have has no sex, no scandal no sizzle to sell the steak. Can you do some miracles like the celebrity magicians reading minds or levitating? Can you do anything that would make you a pop idol? Can you sing your messages, or rap them?"

The prophet was upset by this.

"Does the dream of peace and justice not sell well enough? Does the hope that children can live happy and healthy lives in Africa not have a market?" The prophet was saddened.

"Look, son. I cannot help you. Religion has passed its sell-by date." The guru used body language to signify that the meeting was over.

The prophet left the building. The sign in reception read, "R McGeddon, spreading the word for those who want to profit."

The message is correct, the prophet thought to himself as he walked away.

THE SOCCER TEAM

When we spend our time saving problems from happening we get little credit. When we appear to be only interested in seeking glory through attack we can miss our goals. To be on the winning team we need to keep a balance between the two. Preventing problems and, at the same time, looking for opportunities to score is the best way to move forward.

Tony loved football. He wanted to become as famous as David Beckham. He sought the glory of winning.

His coach was also the team manager and he watched the young lads as they trained. When the time came for team selection, Tony was considered only as the goalkeeper.

The others ran at the same speed as him, they kicked the ball no better than him, but his role would be saving the opponents from scoring. In fact Tony would have been better at striking the ball into the opposition goal than at saving scores in his own.

The team had to rely upon the one position that is the most vulnerable, because they lacked strength in attacking and the defenders were less than perfect.

He never got too much praise for saving. That after all was his job. Perhaps a short lived cheer that was soon forgotten, but he got so much criticism every time he let a ball in. The other players would censure him and blame him for the loss of a game.
He was the one who was so different to the others.

He could handle the ball. He could place the ball before kicking it. He was never seen as part of the winning team. He could only be seen as the man who contributed to a loss.

He had to save penalties given away by other players. He would face the kick as if facing a perverse firing squad and if he caught the ball he survived but if he missed it he died from shame. He carried the weight of poor performances by his team mates.

One day a talent scout came to watch the team play. He studied their attack and defence players but seemed to ignore the goalkeeper.

The shining light of the team, in the view of the coach, was Alan Jones. He ran around to be in the best position for scoring, he passed and received the ball as if playing for a top club.

The talent scout was impressed, yet disappointed that he failed to score.

The scout said "You know, that young striker has no understanding of the role a goalkeeper plays. He does not understand the mindset of that position. Swap them around for five minutes so Alan can get the feel of the weakness of a goalie."

So Alan sulkily got into the mouth of the goal and Tony ran around in the footprints of the potential star.

Tony ran, passed, received and scored. He did it over and over again. Alan stood no chance against him.

After ten minutes the scout asked for the practice game to be stopped.

He scratched his head as he thought. Then he deliberated. He called the coach over.

"You have some talent with these lads but some need to be better trained. Alan looks good. He is flash but he never scored against the goalkeeper, whatever his name is. When the goalkeeper took over as striker he scored a lot of goals, but we would expect that against someone who has never played in the position of goalie. Alan is not good enough to go on yet and the goalkeeper needs more help looking at your results record." He walked away, signing nobody to his books.

Tony had felt the freedom of running and was frustrated that his skills went unnoticed. He left the club and joined a local rugby team. He played at full back where he could defend, attack and use his kicking expertise. A year later he was signed as a bright talent by a major club.

Alan never played for his club again, his heart was broken at the rejection. He felt that had he been a better goal keeper he would have made a greater impression. He could attack but failed to save when under pressure.

He was, however, delighted when the talent scout telephoned him with an offer that would avoid the involvement of the coach and therefore any fees.

He studied the pressures of being a goalkeeper and this knowledge enabled him to spot any weaknesses in the opposing teams he played against. As a result, his ability to score grew dramatically.

He became famous in the game and wanted to be the best in the world. He knew that his attacks would only be as good as the weaknesses of the defence.

Tony progressed and became a rugby star. Both lads had learn a vital lesson that their coach, in those early days, had missed. Preventing problems and, at the same time, looking for opportunities to score is the best way to move forward.

UPDATE

The coaches team was consistently beaten after that day when the two stars left and eventually disbanded.

The talent scout was jailed for taking illicit payments.

EATING AND DRINKING

The very overweight man sat at the table to eat his lunch. He bolted his starter down in just a few moments.

The wine waiter poured out a little bit of fine claret into the man's glass. The man twirled the red liquid, sniffed it, and then analysed the smell. "Merlot with some Cabinet Sauvignon." He said to himself as he nodded his approval to pour more to the waiter.

He took the first sip and probed the flavours with his tongue. He swallowed and allowed the back taste to develop. He took another small sip and put the glass down.

When the main course was served he picked up his knife and fork and set about the meat as if he were a hungry lion. The sautéed potatoes were demolished along with the asparagus.

He sipped his wine again. "Some Pinot Noir in here, as well." He thought.

The man ordered his desert. When it arrived he gobbled it down. He then belched and rubbed his huge stomach as if admonishing it.

A slim and attractive woman, sitting at the adjoining table had watched the whole performance. She had seen him greedily eat his meal yet he had paid so much attention to the wine he had drunk. She had a look of irritation about her face.

She leaned across to the man and asked him if she could say a few things that might make him feel uncomfortable but that would offer him hope.

The man was glad to have the opportunity to converse with such a pretty lady.

"I like riddles, so go ahead." His tone was a mixture of sarcasm and curiosity.

The woman started to speak. "If you ate your food in the same way that you drink your wine, you would be slimmer than you are. When you eat, savour your food as if you were a gourmet. Work out what the chef has used to prepare the food, which spices he has added and the level of seasoning."

The man stared at the woman with a look of surprise.

She continued. "When you eat quickly and without regard for what you are consuming, you will eat more. And when you eat without thinking, you can never value what you have on your plate. That is what has made you overweight. Remember; eat your food with as much ardour as you drink your wine."

With that the woman got up and left.

"Who the heck was she?" The man asked the waiter.

"Oh, her! She is the chef's wife. She loves the skill with which he cooks his food and resents anybody who does not pay enough respect to his efforts. He spent years in different restaurants learning his craft. He studied how herbs and spices work in enhancing the overall flavour and enjoyment of food. He is a true gourmet chef."

Then the waiter asked, "Did you enjoy your meal, sir?"

The overweight man thought about it and replied. "I think so, but I never paid enough attention to what I was eating. The wine was good, though. I think I will start my eating habits tomorrow by coming back to taste the food."

CAVEMEN ON THE BEACH

It seems that when we go on holiday we change. It is as if we travel back in time by 50000 years to revert to the gentler creature that lives inside us when not under threat.

The man looked at the pleasing body of a topless young woman as she stood on the Italian beach. After a while she picked up a T-shirt and pulled it on, covering her bosom. She bent to find a bottle of water in her bag. He found himself peering to see her chest, now mostly hidden. He caught sight of one of her nipples. Even though her breasts had been on full display a few moments earlier, he found that brief glimpse extremely pleasing.

Why was this more interesting than seeing her when she was fully exposed? Was it because he was not supposed to see something that had become private?

Was it because he had broken a taboo by looking at the prohibited?

And was this the great meaning of life? Wanting to see what is hidden and concealed for our own pleasure and amusement? Taking from the universe what is not ours to steal? Having the power not to be punished for breaking the rules? Hoping to glimpse the great secrets of our existence? Wanting to read the last page to see 'who-dun-it' and why?

Perhaps it is the nature of all people to be voyeurs, or at best curious. Maybe it is our curiosity that has driven us for the tens of thousands of years we have survived, rather than lust. This soft-bodied animal without claws, fangs or scaly armour has been able to dominate the fish, birds and every living thing in the world.

It seems that civilisation is only a thin veneer over the primal nature of men. Scratch that surface and you find our real nature underneath

The primal drives that we have are gentle, peaceful and caring. It is so called civilisation that has developed the characteristics that are anything but animal.

Just because a lot of humans can read and write we assume that we have culture. We then assume that culture is a sign of civilisation. The Renaissance followed one of the most troubled periods in European history, the Black Death. However, from that came great works of art in Italy and France, one of the signs of what we call civilisation.

On that beach the man found himself in the middle of a multitude of prehistoric natives. Children played while their parents relaxed. Bare breasted women moved about, or reclined, on the sand. Men in loin cloths paraded, slept or swam. Out to sea, canoes were being paddled in a leisurely way.

This place was a primeval setting, yet it felt safe. Here were nearly naked folk at rest. The clichéd word 'Paradise' emblazoned on a towel summed up the feeling. For two weeks in every fifty two, we find our true, primordial selves. For the other ninety-six percent of the time, we are 'civilised'.

The man and his wife adopted the dress-code by changing into their swimming costumes shyly behind towels wrapped around their pale bodies. 'Are you going topless?' He asked.

Why was he encouraging his wife to show her breasts to strangers? In their ordinary lives back home, he would have punched a Peeping Tom had he peered through the bedroom window from a mile away. Yet here those things, which all men take full possession of, were able to be exposed to a thousand unknown bags of testosterone with the full compliance of the jealous male.

As he tried to rub the sand from his hands, he thought about how much human skin was mixed in with the sand following its natural exfoliation of thousands of people during the season. Athlete's Foot, psoriasis, warts and a multitude of other conditions were also at rest over his towel and his body!

Windsurfers were marooned by the lack of wind. Standing on their boards as if queuing for something, they all appeared to be annoyed that nature had a sense of humour.

There had been enough breeze to take them too far out to swim back and then it weakened to leave them in the doldrums.

The sight was reminiscent of those documentaries where natives stand in canoes whilst spearing fish.

Settling down on his towel, his thoughts turned to how the World might have been fifty thousand years ago when man was a developing force rather than a dominating one. The balance was different. Like a sand castle, the efforts of people would be eroded and taken away by the strength of nature.

Even now those four elements of the Universe are able to dominate. The fire of volcanoes, the water in tidal waves and floods, the earth when split by quakes and the incredible bursts of energy in hurricanes and tornadoes.

When these phenomena occur they treat concrete and steel with the same scant regard that the waves give to a sand-castle. The tsunami that happened in Indonesia, the devastation of New Orleans and the earthquakes in Pakistan were major examples.

Then, church leaders doubted the existence of God because he had not prevented them. Even though they had been brewing for years. Even though cynical insurers called them Acts of God.

Yet those were the very things that had created oceans and mountains millions of years before. They were, and are, the continuing building labourers of our planet.

His thoughts were running at a rapid rate. American, German, Italian and English folk were sharing a beach that a few decades before they would have been fighting each other to possess.

Free from the competition of Nations and dogma, people relaxed under the same sun. The power of politicians and churchmen had divided people for thousands of years.

This predisposition to trust and relax on the beach is an example of the primeval innocence that lives in us when we are not threatened.

Who threatens? The answer seems to be everybody when organised into a hierarchy. Bosses, corporations, governments, nations and churches.

Here they all were, happy to have escaped from their jobs, countries, politicians and civil servants for a while. Perhaps they could relax whilst vulnerable because there was no power base.

Pyramids of power are fairly standard in nature. The alpha males and females dominate the subordinate members of their packs. Sophisticated corporate ladders, political corridors of power, Episcopalian principles rule any collection of people within any organisation. The might of weaponry and armies do the same thing amongst nations.

Pin-stripes, bishops' robes and atom bombs do not make us more civilised than our ancestors. They had muscles, clubs and stones to wield, but that was more for sex and food than absolute control. Gorillas behave with a polite sense of violence. Threaten rather than cause bloodshed.
Civilisation started when mankind got its act together after a very brutal and traumatic birth.

The couple settled down, made the nucleus of their pitch with the umbrellas, and then expanded and protected the zone with towels. This was theirs. Their bits and pieces told others to stay away as strongly as the urine signature of a wolf.

The luxury of being a hunter-gatherer in years-gone-by was that there was always time to relax and chat with your fellows after the prey was caught. In our lives now, hunting and gathering took just moments in the supermarket, so there is time to spent working for others to make their profits.

That means that we never have enough time to sit to relax and chat with friends and family, unless we are on holiday in our loin cloths.

THE METAPHOR OF LIFE AND DEATH

We have ideas about eternity and Heaven but none of really knows what it is like. I guess we will either be ecstatic when our time comes or we will know nothing afterwards if we are unlucky.

Confused and bewildered. Too many colours mixed on a palette. Staggered and hurt. I was dead. I saw my body beneath me. Tubes and bandages. Flowers in a vase wilting as if acknowledging my demise. Nurses and doctors resigning themselves to yet another loss. I could hear them muttering as they sped off to another emergency.

Rather than floating up a shaft of light into a celestial palace, it was like being turned into a piece of space smaller than the size of a bubble in a bottle of tonic water.

No ancestors waiting to greet me as if my death was a surprise birthday party. Thank goodness for that! Not that I had anything against my ancestors but I wanted the afterlife to be something different to the cliché we are fed upon.

Dying was not what I thought it would be. I was still alive but out of touch with my body, my vehicle for so many years. Now I was living in a different place with extra bits. Time lost its threat and became another facet of the diamond.

I had assumed that I would be fixed in age, my wish would have been to be 32. Instead I was ageless. I was newborn and an old man all in one. I was able to revisit points in my life at the ages I was when they happened.

I could see my parents as they had been when I was a five year old about to embark upon my first day at school or as a grandfather on my sixtieth birthday.

It was weird. I was experiencing as well as seeing and hearing everything.

I used my memories to move around in time. I kissed my first true love again. That first time I had felt somebody else's tongue in my mouth. It was real rather being a memory or daydream.

I relived my first kiss that I did not enjoy out of curiosity. I had forgotten it as a man but now I could smell the strawberry flavoured chewing gum on the girl. Now it had come back to me as if I had found something in the bottom of a filing cabinet. Something that had fallen down the back rather than had been destroyed.

This is not the right place to recall losing my virginity, but I lost it so many times, as it happened, in my new world, or universe. I could replay and replay as many times as I wanted in my little bubble of this new existence.

Well I say bubble, but it was different to that. I recalled the time I had visited a zoo and had watched, God like, as leaf-cutter ants scurried along clear plastic pipes. They had no awareness of me, and the other people, watching. They were in their own world. I was now like one of those ants but able to scamper about and watch the others at the same time, but without a sense of time. I was a man and a deity at the same time.

Being able to experience things without limbs was strange. It was different to paralysis where you could think without being able to move. The sad parts of my life could be skipped track by track as if playing a DVD with many parts. This was strange. My emotions still worked and I could live through my life over and over again. The tragedies compelled me to re-live them but frustration crept in as I was unable to change the circumstances.

Yet I enjoyed sitting on my grandfather's lap over and over again. I enjoyed eating my paternal grandmother's apple pie and my maternal grandmother's fried new potatoes. Every time it was a new experience relived.

This was a different Heaven to the one we hear about from those who have never been there. I could watch films over and over. I could go to places and events that I had never experienced. I attended Elvis, Pavarotti, Maria Callas and Beatles concerts for the first time and sat through my repeats. It was truly wonderful.

As I was the container of all my experiences, I also revisited my dreams. Those that I remembered and those that I had forgotten. Nightmares could be seen as horrific stories full of scary things, but knowing that I was safe helped me to experience them as I did when visiting theme parks. A danger that is known to be totally safe lacks menace. A buzz from the achievement of experiencing peril was satisfying.

Some repeated dreams that I had when alive were

there in full view and in full colour. My living dreams seemed to go to the same places. One was always in France, on the side of a mountain where I would meet up with my friends and drink wine and laugh. This place existed in this new realm, but some of my friends were missing. I could visit them on Earth, but they had not yet left on this journey, and the future was as resistant to penetration as it had been in the past. I guessed that when their little holograms came here we would complete the scene, and I was right.

Caught up by my nostalgia and my self-indulgence I was unable to expand in this place.

After a while, excuse the expression because there was no sense of time in this existence, I was able to see the essences of other people and things. If I call these little bubbles souls, that makes it easier to talk about. They were everywhere, the souls of people, animals, plants and minerals. How could they all fit?

They were as abundant as raindrops in a monsoon, as plentiful as droplets of water in a thick fog, yet there was space. The infinity of molecules of water in the oceans must have been greater than all the after-lives I encountered, yet they all fitted, and that was within the confines of the planet, and we were in the greater infinity of the Universe!
They, we, floated around as if splendid butterflies.

Beautiful containers of the memories of experience as if they were colours of the darkest and lightest shades.

It was a bagatelle. I bounced off people, other animals, plants and minerals. All those things that had experienced a life on Earth.

I could tap into their experiences as well. I realised that they could tap into mine. Here was a concept of good and evil, decent and bad. The others could see the time when I had stolen my cousin's toy car. Worse they could see...well I am not confessing everything here. Perhaps this was the sense of judgment that we had guessed at on Earth. The punishment was being so transparent to other souls.

I could experience how it was to fight wars and to be killed in them. I knew how it was to make peace and to save lives. This was the true eternity of infinity. I could be a fish or a bird or a lion. I could be a snake, a monkey or a kitten. I could be an oak tree or a mountain.

The future, well the future in our terrestrial definition, was difficult at first. Unable to visit it as if using a time-machine, I sought the bubbles of memory from the future and the past and shared their lives. It was like visiting the largest library that could be imagined, and then more.

The essence of the end of the world was there, narrated by the last people to live as humans. It had not affected them, they were still floating around because they were somewhere other than on the planet.

We could float anywhere in this infinity. We could tour the Grand Canyon; we could plumb the depths of the Pacific Ocean. We could visit the planets, we could be in different galaxies too different to be easy to describe in the words of the Earth.

It is difficult even to use words to explain how it was.

We are as collective as the experiences of the others that I had viewed and those things became part of my experience and were viewed by others. This meant that I became closer and closer to having undergone everything that had ever happened and would happen. I was expanding to be an amalgam of all experiences and as this happened I became more and more remote from my individuality, my ego.

This was the collective unconsciousness of all forms of life on Earth. Then we drifted through time and space on the next part of this journey through the infinity of the universe.

Earth was of a smaller proportion than a single cell in the body of an elephant. There were so many more things to share with the souls of the infinite.

INTRODUCTION TO FANTASIES AND DREAMS
(Interactive metaphors)

Dreams are so annoying. They tell stories, alter moods and then dissolve away, leaving you with the frustrations of not being able to remember them.

Attempts to recall dreams are reminiscent of those times when we have tried to pull earthworms from their holes. You get a small grip and then they slip away to hide. Later they might come out fully, but only rarely.

Perhaps dreams take us to a different universe. One that can offer pleasure and one that can offer horror. People, alive and dead, come into that world. People we have lost contact with will appear with monotonous regularity.

We can see things that are invisible in our waking moments, we can hear and smell beautiful and ugly things.

We can fantasise in our dreams, we can set goals for ourselves and hope that when our dream universe merges back into our waking lives, those dreams come true.

Enjoy the following Fantasies and Dreams. They will relax and sooth you, help you to visualise and give you a sense of optimism. They are purposely told to the reader so that they are interactive. The page talks to you directly when you wish to listen

AUTUMN LEAVES

You are taking a brisk walk through a wood on a fine autumn afternoon. The ground is covered with a layer of fallen leaves, crackling and rustling under your feet.

Through the leaves you can see the sky, which is a deeper blue than you have ever seen before.

Although the leaves are piling up on the path, making it barely visible, the branches of the trees are still dotted with leaves: some a golden yellow, some a rich orange, and others a vivid red.

You can feel a slight chill in the air but you are warmed by the radiance of the colours that surround you. You can feel a glow within you that reflects the colours of the leaves. Golden for the goals you want to achieve, orange for your energy to work towards them, and red for your courage to overcome your doubts.

You are still walking, but your steps are becoming slower. Although you know you must make progress, you also know that sometimes it is necessary to stop and look around you. You feel, with increasing certainty, that now is one of those times.

You pause.

This must be the oldest part of the wood. Immense trees stretch up towards the sky on either side of you.

A maze of cracks covers the bark of the nearest tree

trunk and as you look more closely you can see pale green lichen growing along the ridges.

The bark looks as if it would crumble away if you touched it, but when you place your hand on the tree, it feels as hard and as steadfast as granite. The cracks are not a display of weakness; instead, they are channels of strength. Lower down the trunk there are pockets of moss and you brush your fingers over them. You expect the moss to feel slimy and damp, but it is dry and feathery to your touch.

As you stand near the tree a sense of age and timelessness seems to seep out from it, as though it is sending a message through your fingertips into your deepest levels of understanding.

It is as if the wisdom of the ancient philosophers, of the magicians of mythology, and even of our own ancestors, is collected together and preserved in the life of the tree.

You look down at the base of the tree. Powerful roots spread out in all directions, like buttresses, supporting and nourishing the tree. You know that the roots spread out for the same distance as the height of the tree, and, just for a moment, you imagine you can see them beneath the ground, reaching out for water and nutrients, dividing and becoming increasingly finer as they extend deeper and further out in their search to sustain the tree.

You look up and see the branches reaching upwards with serenity and confidence, mirroring the structure of the roots as they divide and spread out in search of the sunlight.

Above you a branch trembles in the breeze, and a leaf gently detaches itself and flutters down to the ground. Another leaf follows, and another. In only a few weeks from now, the tree's branches will be bare. In your imagination you can see time moving forward through the winter and on to the spring, and you see buds forming on the branches of the trees, then swelling, opening and breaking out into fresh young leaves, and you realise that none of this would happen if the tree did not give up its old leaves in the autumn.

You think of the things in your life that you would like to let go: things you do not want to do any longer, your negative thoughts, and everything that is stopping you from being the person you would like to be.

The tree is shedding its leaves because it is the right time for it to do so. You feel that it is the right time for you, too, to shed the things you would like to see gone from your life. And you can feel them breaking off, one by one, floating downwards, away from you, leaving you free to pursue new activities, to enjoy positive thoughts, to become how you would like to be.

An exhilarating feeling of freedom fills your mind, as you realise that from now on there is no need for these things to be part of your life any longer.

SUMMERHOUSE HILL

You have arrived in a field. And the morning is cold. Grey clouds of fog are hanging in the air, bringing a clinging dampness with them. Yesterday your ambition was to walk to the top of Summerhouse Hill.

Today you have your doubts, however. The path is wet and slippery and the summit seems so far away. You feel no enthusiasm for this trek at all. It might be easier to stay where you are. But it's damp and depressing here, so you reluctantly decide to carry on.

Your rucksack is heavy, as if it contained all of your troubles and cares. The prospect of the walk is troubling you, but you plod on. The mud seems to be pulling your feet backwards, the slope tries to push you back to where you came from. The air is thick and your dark thoughts weigh you down as much as the load on your back.

As you trundle along, you see the outlines of trees and bushes in the distance, disguised by the mist, to look like monsters lurking in the gloom. Their natural green changed to a sombre dark mass.

You continue upwards, and as you do so the air seems to be thinning, and you become aware that the grass by the side of the path is looking brighter; an infrequent flower appears to be rubbing its eyes to welcome the day ahead. The mud is less thick, less sticky, and as if to help you, an occasional bird sings to you.
As you progress, ever upwards, the mist is thinning

to a haze now, and so much more is visible. You can see trees and bushes in detail; red, blue and yellow flowers. The path stretching out in front of you into a small clump of trees. The path almost beckons you forward, rather than holding you back.

You're feeling better now, and you're feeling happy that you decided to continue with your plans. Where you are now is better than from whence you came; the initial discomfort makes what you have now feel even better than perhaps it might have been if you had started with the sun shining on you. Perhaps the gloom was a spur to move up to these greater heights.

You're nearly at the trees now, the birdsong louder and more melodic, and the air cleaner and clearer. You enter the trees and just ahead you notice a small deer grazing, oblivious to your presence; or perhaps it's just not frightened by you.

You stop to watch and as you do, it occurs to you that this is like a comparison with your life. You know that if you chased at the deer, if you tried to get too close, too quickly, it would run away. Perhaps if you stand still the deer will continue to graze, move even closer to you. And you think of some of the things that you have stopped by being too eager, things that you have lost by wanting to possess them too quickly. Things like relationships, even your sleep, and your own satisfaction.

You see that the deer turns to look at you, nods its head up and down as if in agreement with your thoughts, and then it wanders slowly away into the thicker part of the woods to continue feeding. And you are left with a sense of peace and enlightenment. You continue with your journey, aware of little scufflings as life gets on with its business.

At the end of this arcade of trees, as the sunlight greets you, there is so much more of a spring in your step, your head is held higher, the rucksack on your back thought of as a container for pleasant necessities for your trip, rather than as an encumbrance. The sun adds its warmth to the mood of this improving day. You feel good, you feel wonderful as you continue upwards towards what you now see as an obtainable goal. The slope is taken in your stride.

You realise that nothing much has changed. Apart from your perception of what was always around you. The hill, the woods, the animals, the plants and flowers; the day itself; are all as they were before. You are the same person that you were before, but you are thinking in a new way. You are seeing life so much more clearly, you are aware of everything in a different way.

As you reach the top of the hill, the day is so warm, so comfortable. The sky is a deep blue and the sun highlights the colours around you; different shades of green, the sharp strong shadows thrown by the trees, flowers of all hues reaching down into the valley below, where you can see the bright sparkle of a stream as it meanders along.
The view from the summit is magnificent. Other hills rolling away, stretching into the distance, and boasting a patchwork of fields, hedges, and small forests. Every so often you notice buildings nestled

together in small villages. Sometimes many buildings making towns. It as if the whole world can be seen from here.

You absorb the sights, the sounds, the smells and mix them with the way you feel, to make an experience that is rich in the joy of being alive, of being able to be part of everything that exists. You feel wonderful, invigorated by this encounter with life, the life that is all around you.

You realise that this feeling would not have been there for you if you had given up at the bottom, if the desire to climb out of the gloom had not been strong enough. The greyness has been replaced by bright colours, the coldness by warmth, and the burdens by lightness. All of this arose from your decision to change your life and circumstances, the decision to improve what you had before.

You turn to start your descent, walking slowly back down, through the trees, through this wonderful sunshade of leaves and branches. The deer is there again, this time aware of you approach. It seems to nod its approval of the way you feel, as if it shows in your smile, your manner and your sense of ease. This feeling will last for ever, no matter what happens in your life.

You continue downwards, the path dry now and easy to walk upon. Soon you are back. It is different, the greyness you left behind has given way to brightness.

You know that you have returned to where you started from, but it is no longer what it was. It is a starting point for a new way for you to look at your life in a positive way; and in the future it can be a starting point for a fresh climb up the hill to those glorious sights, sounds and feelings. But as you look around you realise that the biggest difference is, you.

PALACE OF DREAMS

You are in the entrance hall of a grand palace. You know that this is the palace of your fantasies, daydreams and your sleeping dreams.

On the walls are paintings depicting you in various situations that you have enjoyed in your life.

Magnificent paintings that are so lifelike that they are like huge cinema screens that have been frozen. In between these paintings is a closed door that leads into a special room. Every room in this gigantic palace is a part of your imagination where you can play and feel part of every fantasy that you have ever wanted, and even those that you have not even thought of before.

This is a place where you can plan the fantasies that you will have, and that you will remember, adding people, scenes and actions as you wish. Here you can become whatever you want to be, be wherever you want to be, and be doing whatever you want to do.

You are aware that this palace is really your own mind, you can become whatever you set your mind to becoming, you can fulfil that rich inner potential by self-belief, by seeing what you want to become. You know that your potential is as infinite as the universe, as benevolent as it should be, to yourself and to others.

A fantasy can be reliving old memories, perhaps changing some of the details in order to obtain a different outcome. A fantasy can also be a reality that has not, as yet, occurred. Help those fantasies, believe in them and achieve what you want.

You have been to this palace before, you can see the splendour of the buildings. You see the doors to the numerous rooms, each of which contains a scenario and cast for your fantasy.

And you choose a door, perhaps one that you have been through before, perhaps a new one. You decide in advance. You decide now. Perhaps you will leave it to your own imagination to suddenly present a scene to you as you walk through a mystery door.

Step through whichever door you have chosen…now.

Notice everything that you can about the place, are you in a room, a building, a town; or are you in the open air; is it flat, hilly, mountainous; what can be seen, who is there with you?

Add the detail for yourself, as if you were painting a grand masterpiece. But in this masterpiece you can add the temperatures that surround you. Is it hot or cool? You can add the smells and the textures of the things that you are adding. You can change the time-scale from present to future or back into the past.

So find yourself in that scene now and enjoy your fantasy.

STOP READING AND START DREAMING, NOW
And now relax and let yourself return to the entrance hall of the palace. You can see the painting that you

drew earlier, hanging in its place beside the door that you entered before.

When you are ready, return to this page.

You are looking forward to the next time that you visit this wonderful palace, your own imagination.

ISLAND

And now you feel as if your mind is just floating through time and space, travelling faster and faster, travelling further and further, until you arrive gently on a beautiful tropical island beach. You can see and feel the white sand beneath your feet. You can see and hear the sea gently rolling onto the shore.

The beach seems to stretch for ever, curving away from you in both directions until it is lost behind the palm trees that skirt the island. You are aware that you are the only person on the beach, the only person on the island. You can hear the gurgling of the pebbles as the waves roll in, stirring the water's edge.

The foam flicks into you face, cooling you in this pleasant warmth from the sun. You reflect on how good you feel as the sun gives its warmth, kindly, to every element of your body.

You feel safe, you somehow know that every plant, every animal and every part of this island is safe. You know that this place exists to help you to feel better and better about yourself. It is a sanctuary where you can relax and feel at ease.

As with yourself, you are aware that this island has more to offer, a much greater potential, and you are eager to explore and to discover that potential.

You turn to look inland, and you notice a small stream trickling gently from the forest that stretches beyond the palm trees. You decide to follow that little river into the forest.

You walk along a small path beside the water. You are feeling wonderful as you gaze at the greens of the forest, some dark, some light, some bright where the sun is shining on the leaves. Fingers of bright sunlight are reaching through the branches as if they were trying to gently wrap themselves around you in a tender, caring way. The water of the stream babbles and chatters, as if it alive, almost as if it contains the very spirit of life itself.

Soon you reach a small gentle waterfall. Beneath the shower of water, the pool looks so welcoming, it seems to beckon you in. You know, somehow that this pool will wash away so many of your problems, so many of your cares. You dip your fingers into the pond and it feels so warm, so welcoming.

You are alone and you start to undress, there is nobody there to see you. You feel so free as you remove your clothes item by item, leaving them in a pile by the bank of the stream.

Gently lower yourself into the crystal clear water, first your feet, then your ankles, calves and your thighs.

The pool is shallow and you sit on the bottom, letting the water cover your stomach and chest. You lay back and float, feeling so safe and secure. You feel as if the water is dissolving every worry that you ever had, every care, every piece of self-doubt. You dip your head under the warm cascade, bursting back out again in a blissful splash, all of you feeling light and wonderful as all of those uncertainties are washed away. Your cares just seem to float away and disappear downstream, never to return again, floating away into that huge ocean that you saw earlier, to be diluted over and over again so that they can never be reformed.

You feel so excited that you want to explore more and more of this wonderful, almost magical place. You leave the water and instantly dry in the warmth of the sun. You abandon your clothes and walk naked, as if newly born, further upstream.

Very soon you see another waterfall feeding another pool of warm, welcoming water. This one seems to be different. There is a subtle aura of light; different colours playing on the surface, reflecting the sunshine, the different shades of the forest.

You walk gently into this part of the stream, lowering yourself smoothly. This pond seems full of the essence of optimism, full of hope, ambition and desire. These elements appear to penetrate your every cell, every nerve in your body and mind. You feel so elated, so invigorated, so uplifted.

Again, you stand beneath the gentle shower of water, enjoying this feeling of optimism, this feeling of inner strength. You rest there for a while, enjoying this feeling of refreshment, of liberation.

This time as you leave the water, the droplets remain, as if they were continuing to soak into your very being rather than evaporating away.
You see a beautiful robe and you put it on. You continue to walk along that stream, along that path until eventually, you see a clearing in the forest, the sun dappling down through the trees, it's looking tranquil and wonderful.

You lay on a soft bed of moss and grass and you begin to doze off into a pleasant and restful sleep. As you sleep you dream that every one of those water droplets is a positive thought that will change the way in which you now face the challenges of your life.

You know that these thoughts will stay with you as you return to the reality of your life. You know how you will benefit from being refreshed and revitalised, how you will gain from an optimistic outlook.

THE PARK

Autumnal browns, greens and golds from the leaves of the trees pervade the scene. And although there's a slight chill in the air, you're feeling comfortable and serene, reflecting somehow the majestic ambience that surrounds you. This is peace, stillness and tranquillity; this is perfect calmness.

The trees you see there are old, solid and they seem wise somehow. And the bark on their trunks looks like the old skin of figures of wisdom, the sages, the mythological magicians, our own ancestors, perhaps. It is as if they have grown from the strengths of all of those things that have ever existed, perhaps from those things and people whose very natures have been kept alive by this different form of life.

They have had contact with the depths of the earth, their roots searching and exploring every nook and cranny, finer roots speeding off in search of water and nourishment.

Their branches becoming finger like twigs reaching and stretching into the sky, carrying leaves which, in turn, absorb the energy of the sun.

These trees have connection with every part of life, every part of the world; air, water, earth and the fire, the warmth of the sun itself.

They stand, serene and gentle, yet strong and able to withstand the onslaught of fierce winds, driving rain; the encounters with animals, birds and insects.
In a small clearing, you become aware of a trickling,

gurgling noise, a spring of fresh, clear and clean water. The water spills out into a very small pool before overflowing and disappearing back down into the earth.

Three big noble trees seem to be pointing down to the pool as if drawing your attention to it. It seems significant, it seems special. The wisdom of the trees beckons you to do something, to feel something.

Perhaps there is a magic in this place, in this water. You sit by the water, feeling so relaxed, so content. You drift into time and space as if these things were moving forwards and backwards, speeding up and slowing down, twisting and turning.

The bubbles that play on the surface as the water bursts out, fascinate you, they seem to hypnotise you as they reflect the colours that surround this place, as they reflect and blend in the sunlight, and the movement of the trees and grasses around this oasis of wisdom.

And as you look a leaf from the first tree drops gently down into the water. And in the middle of the pond, there is a patch, a clear patch, that reflects your face distinctly, but reflecting your life as it is at this moment.

Then a leaf from the second tree drops down into the water, making little ripples. As this happens you can see yourself as you were when you were very young, the look of surprise and optimism on your face, the joy and anticipation as you looked forward to the future with all your dreams and hopes.

It is as if the slight disturbance in the surface of the water move time itself, around and around. But as the water moves slightly you're aware that the movements of space and time are caught up in that reflection. And as time swirls around you can sense the differences between then and now, how the world has treated you, how you have treated the world.

Perhaps you feel satisfaction at some aspects of your life, and you're aware of what they are, perhaps you feel disappointment with other things.

A leaf from the third tree then falls down into the pond and you know that this pool shows the future as well as the past and the present. You can see yourself as you would be if you continued with the same style of life that you currently lead, but you can also see yourself as you would be if you changed. And you can see the way you want to be and sense the way you want to feel. And you can experience that now.

You explore the possibilities, compare the ways in which you would be if life were different. And you can see what makes you different in the future, what makes you more confident, more successful, and happier.

You reach into the pond to pick up those three leaves, and you notice that they all look the same as each other. The difference is the way they have reflected your life, the three ages of your life, what you have had, what you have and what you might have.

Now, you are sitting on a low brick wall beside a stream. The stream is flowing so slowly that you can hardly see the water move. On the surface of the water tiny insects dart about, too small and too fast for you to see, but you can see the ripples and little disturbances they leave behind.

From time to time, the stream shimmers as a light breeze brushes across it, creating a new pattern for a few moments, until the tranquillity of the surface is restored once more. The water is clear, so clear that you can see right to the bottom of the stream: you can see the light brown mud, the outlines of water plants, the smooth stones. You feel yourself relaxing in sympathy with the unhurried pace of the stream.

There are trees on each side of the stream and you can see their shadows on the surface of the water. You can see straight and unwavering shadows of tree trunks, but also you can see small patches and narrow bands of shade from the leaves and branches of the trees. These dance over the water with the breeze, forming patterns of darkness and light, which merge briefly and then divide again.

As you deepen your gaze, you realise you can see more than shadows; you can see the reflections of the trees. At first you find it hard to look through the shadows down to the images below them, but as you continue to look, the whole scene reveals itself to you.

Whereas the shadows of the leaves were fuzzy and blurred, the reflections of the leaves are sharp and defined. You can see all the colours in the water: the light green of the oak leaves contrasting with the dark grey-green of the pine leaves. Through the tops of the trees you can see the clear blue of the sky. As the surface of the water moves, the reflections dissolve and re-form before your eyes.

You move closer to the water and you can now see your own shadow, a silhouette of your head, neck and shoulders. You shift the focus of your gaze, looking deeper into the water, and now you can see your face distinctly reflected below you. But something is happening to the water: it is becoming agitated, with small waves rippling outwards. You continue to watch, entranced by the pictures coming in and out of view. It seems that time itself is caught up in the movement of the water and is swirling around and over you. Just for a moment, a calm patch forms in the midst of the turbulence, and you see your face as it was when you was a child.

The eyes looking up at you are shining with the hopes and dreams that you once had. As the ripples in the surface spread across the water, you imagine the ripples spreading outwards from the image you had of your childhood. The water swirls once more and the vision disappears, but the memory of how you once were is still there with you. Perhaps some of your aspirations have been realised; perhaps some have changed; perhaps some have persisted all through your life and you are still waiting to achieve them.

You wonder what the result of making changes to your life might be, and, as if echoing your thoughts, the water clears once more, showing more pictures.

You see yourself as you would be if you continued to

live your life as you do at present, but also you see yourself as you would be if you changed. As you look at the pictures, you feel yourself relaxing more, and you find that you are able to let yourself experience, here and now, how you want to be, how you want to feel in the future.

You take a smooth round stone from the bank of the stream, and hold it in the palm of your hand. It is cool to your touch and you feel mysteriously reassured by its weight. As you hold the stone in your hand, you explore the opportunities you have to make changes, to achieve your dreams, to become more confident, more successful, and more content.

The harmony and the tranquillity of the scene are drawing you into a feeling of perfect calmness and peace. Feeling so relaxed now, you lower your hand down to the surface of the stream, open your fingers and, very gently, slip the stone into the water. It sinks down to the bottom, and as you see it descend through the water, you can feel confidence and strength sinking into your own mind, slipping through the barrier of your conscious thoughts, and continuing right down to the deepest levels.

You realise that this feeling is here to stay, and that the changes you want to make are already beginning to happen, and will continue until you achieve your vision of how you want to be.

PLANET

You are travelling through space and time to the surface of a distant planet, a planet similar to the Earth, with a rich atmosphere, and the absence of all negative thoughts and actions.

Here you are, as light as the air and you can choose to walk or float in perfect safety. This is a place where you, as your ideal self, have fulfilled every wish and hope that you wanted to achieve on Earth, but were unable to because of the way you felt, or through poor circumstances, or bad luck, or, whatever.

Here, the sun is warm, the water pure, the air is clean and invigorating. You decide to float, to explore, to experience this New World. Drifting through space, you can see huge mountains that shimmer in the bright sunlight, green plants and fruit laden trees. You can see animals that acknowledge you floating above them, seeming to look up and smile as you pass overhead.

You do not know why, but every sound, every sight, every smell of the life around you fills you with the essence of this place, optimism, hope and confidence. You are aware that this place is unselfish, it exists for you, and therefore you exist for it. You have a feeling that what you do to help this place will be returned to you in terms of your happiness, your tranquillity, and your fulfilment. How you wish that Earth could be like this.

Gently and gradually, a place appears beneath you, it a situation that you recognise as familiar from your life on Earth, that has caused you to feel that life has had more to offer; it could be your work, your house, your partner, your possessions, your emotions, your health, your habits; perhaps a mixture of some, or all, of those things. This place is so familiar to you. But it is different.

Rather than possessing the negatives that are so well-known to you, the place is full of positives. The differences are so marked that you can see what would have to change in order to transform one to the other. You can see yourself as you could be, your circumstances as they would be.

Slowly you descend, slowly descend, towards this location, ready to experience, rather than witness; ready to be involved in the different happenings, the different moods, the different feelings.

Floating down, you realise that you are here in spirit only, the substance of you is living life as it is most desirable, you are watching this other you, noticing the subtle differences, examining how a changed attitude could make so much improvement to every aspect of your life.

You can experience the benefits if that turnabout took place, if you tried to emulate that alternative you, if you used your encounter with that alternative you to improve your own quality of life.

You approach your alternative self, who is aware of your presence, and ask, "What is the secret to the much better quality of life that I can sense?"

You are told that you should travel this world and list

the positive attributes that you behold, and then compare them with the negatives that have pervaded life on Earth. Then you are told to return at a later time with the conclusion that you have come to. The alternative self then turns around with a wry and knowing smile.

Disappointed that you have to do the work, rather than be given the answer, you tell yourself to float back into the air, thinking that this is a silly riddle that you will never be able to solve.

Then it occurs to you as you float upwards that the first part of the answer has already been given. The negative feeling that you had about having to do and think things out for yourself showed ingratitude.

Perhaps the positive attitude should have been one of appreciation. The realisation that a negative feeling came to you before a positive thought comes as an insight. The alternative self was trying to help you rather than exploit you. Helping others to benefit is a more positive way to live rather than by exploiting them.

As you float, the sun is warm like an emotion, warmth rather than coldness, love rather than hate. Another answer.

The water pure rather than corrupt, the air is clean and invigorating rather than choking and restricting. Drifting through space, you can see huge mountains that shimmer in the bright sunlight, beautiful green plants and fruit laden trees that seem to have existed for ever. The trees give their fruit in exchange for the insects and animals pollinating their flowers and spreading their seeds. They seem satisfied that they have received in return for giving. In return for giving the insects and animals have also received. Yet another answer; satisfaction rather than greed.

You can see the animals that acknowledge you floating above them, seeming to look up and smile as you pass overhead. Integration rather than rejection.

It becomes easier and easier. Motivation to find the answer, to achieve something is preferable to being envious of those who already know. Involvement in life itself is more satisfying than trying to escape from its problems by the use of drink or drugs. Here, a sense of achievement replaces self-criticism.

Drifting back and downwards to your alternative self, you feel a sense of pride and satisfaction that you have found the solution to your worries and cares. It is not the place you are in, it is not the circumstances that you find; it is rather the way in which you perceive and react to the way things are. Find the positive side to every situation rather than accept the negatives. Rather than change the way things are, change yourself, and then those things that have upset and worried you will seem to change themselves.

You greet your alternative self with enthusiasm, you can see that your return is welcomed. Your conclusion is the insight that you wanted. This is the same place that Earth is, everything is identical, except that you had perceived everything in a negative way. Of course it is the same place. The difference is you. But now, you are different, you are positive.

Now you know why every sound, every sight, every smell of the life around you fills you with the essence of this place, optimism, hope and confidence. You are aware that this place is unselfish, it exists for you, and therefore you exist for it.

You have a feeling that what you do to help this place will be returned to you in terms of your happiness, your tranquillity, and your fulfilment. How you wished that Earth could be like this.

Your wish has come true.

LANDSCAPE PAINTING

The landscape stretches as far as the eye can see.

Changes of blue in the sky give the impression that the sky is like big lid over this beautiful scene. There are a few clouds; a mixture of white fluffy ones, darker chunky ones, their bases darker than the tops, that are highlighted by the sunshine, seeming to float.

The sun is so bright now, sharp shadows emphasize the features. In the bright landscape, you are aware of the darker shadows where the clouds hover between the land and the sun. You can see the undulation of the land, the sharper greens cutting off the darker ones.

Hills rise out of flat landscape, as if they want to see everything around them. White chalk paths work their way to the tops of some. Occasionally there are bigger bowls of chalk where the ground has slipped away.

Farmers' fields look like the felt on a snooker table from a distance the smooth texture of carefully tended crops.

Small birds scuttle around, contributing sounds that seem to come from everywhere. Flowers add different colours to the grasses; dandelions and daisies, bluebells and gorse, buttercups, purple flowers, cow parsley.

A bird of prey is hovering, fluttering its wings, waiting for its prey that takes cover in clumps of tall grasses.

Black and white cows are grazing in a large field, and in another, closer field you can see the creamy shapes of sheep, contrasting with the white of the young lambs. There are dots of black as crows peck at insects disturbed by the sheep.

You realise as you look at ploughed fields that ground that is brown doesn't always mean that it is sterile or barren, it can be fertile and full of life waiting to burst out.

There is a slow river laying in the grassy knolls, lined by stunted willow trees reaching over the water, weeds sitting in the middle of the water. Shrubs are reflected on the still water.

You can see forests and small woods in patches. You notice that the smaller trees are on the outside; the innermost trees grow higher to get the light, they are taller. Dark shadows make arches and alleyways at the entrance to those wooded areas, sometimes foreboding, sometimes welcoming, depending on the intensity of the darkness. Sometimes crows are perched at the tops of trees like black blobs, swaying in the wind. All the trees are bursting into leaf.

Where the trees appear on the tops of the ridges and hills in the landscape they are bent over by the wind, as if held in that shape as they grew, leaning away from the wind, fluffy tops stretching out, like fingers pointing away from the wind as if reaching for something strong and stable to hold onto. It reminds you of the expression from your childhood that you'll stay like that if the wind changes.

In other places you notice ivy growing up through

trees, brambles through hedges, as if these weaker plants were using the strength of others to end up in a much better position.

Sometimes there are trees in avenues, sometimes in clumps. Some are old, some are young and fresh. Some have fallen by the wayside, laying on the ground like slumbering large animals, wooden sculptures. There are some trees that seem to be like giants surrounding and protecting small villages.

The houses in these villages display different colours of stones highlighting their individuality. Some with white window frames and black door frames. Some have roses growing up cottages as if to reach the thatch. Some have smoke rising lazily from the chimneys.

Spires of churches reach above the trees, as if watching over the houses nearby. An old inn makes you think of log fires and foaming jugs of ale being passed around as in the old days when these villages were young. People and nature in harmony.

This picture that you have seen is perfection. Explore it with your mind for a few minutes.

Look at every aspect of your life as if describing a painting to a blind person.

RIVER BANK

You're in the countryside, beside a gently flowing small river. A path stretches out in front of you and you're just strolling along.

The sun is beginning to break through the hazy clouds, its warmth becoming noticeable on your forehead. It's comfortable and it's pleasant. There's a stillness in the air, the leaves on the trees hardly moving. The faint scent of the foliage is an agreeable perfume that permeates the atmosphere in a gentle and amiable way.

Birds are singing and chirping; and you can see them sometimes, gliding between the trees and bushes, sometimes hopping from branch to branch.

And by the side of the path you can see grasses and wild plants, enjoying the opportunity to show their green leaves to the sun, absorbing that natural energy, preparing to burst into activity after the long Winter slumber. And here and there flowers are showing themselves to passers-by, to creatures that will help them to create the next generation; to admirers. They almost seem to be boasting to each other. "I'm brighter than you. I'm prettier than you."

The track in front of you meanders with the river, no rush to get anywhere, just taking pleasure from the journey. It seems lazy, but it has its purpose; it will get to its destination, but, in its own time. Within this seeming lethargy, you can sense an energy, a hidden energy which suggests that it's strong but controlled, showing itself only when needed. You can see a large stone in the middle of the stream.

The energy shows itself as foaming waves, babbling and chattering, pushing on one side, sucking and pulling on the other.

And you know that over time, the time that it takes, that stone will be smoothed and worn away; it will be dealt with. What was once an obstacle will become just a memory. And as soon as the water has passed that obstacle by, the stream will reform, it will become as it was; still and quiet, peaceful and easy.

In the same fashion, you're aware of the stored vigour in the plants around you, the buds preparing to burst into life, with new leaves, stronger branches, flowers, and seeds.

Meanwhile, the birds are busy making territories and nests; and life itself.

So, you are part of this as an essential element of life, as an observer, and as a participant. It is as if everything that you see, hear, smell, feel and sense is only there because you are there to witness it, as if you are the essential ingredient for the existence of all these things.

But the force of nature that you are experiencing is part of you, your will is as unstoppable as the water in the river, as determined to flourish as every plant that you see, as resolved as every bird you can see and hear, to make your place and destiny. But more so.

You can recognise the potential that you have. It can be used in a conscious way rather than by instinct. You're aware that you can change the way in which you do things.

You know that sometimes that potential is forgotten, sometimes ignored. However it is always there, a store of experiences, some good, some bad; but experiences are the different ways in which new things were done then; the way that you thought the best at the time; and sometimes in hindsight those ways proved to be the best, sometimes those things could have been done in a different way. No matter what you did, you learnt, you gained knowledge that helped, and will help you in future situations.

As you progress along the path, the sun is even warmer and more comfortable, the path smoother and easier to walk and you feel more and more relaxed, more and more at ease with the life you have. You feel more and more confident, that pool of knowledge having become larger and larger.

You see a bench by the side of the river, it looks soft and inviting. A small voice inside your head tells you that you would be lazy to sit here.

The voice tells you to continue, to rush ahead, to get to where you are going in the fastest possible time.

It tells you that anybody who sees you sitting will think you idle, the plants and animals will think you slothful. There is pressure to keep going on, to avoid sitting down. But you want to sit, nevertheless this voice keeps nagging you to go on, to keep pushing yourself. And you're feeling confused.

You decide to sit for a short while, to compromise. As you sit you stare into the water, shapes swirling, changing, depending on where you look, sometimes into the depths, sometimes at the surface. Pictures form and you can see the past and the future. The river always looks the same but it's ever changing.

The water that is passing now has come from the past, but the water that is passing is moving into the future. You can see a vision of what the river will see when it travels on for a while. You can see the path on the bank littered with people who have listened to that voice which condemned them for wanting to rest.

They kept on going, fearful of criticism, fearful of failure. They ignored their own needs, they wanted to reach that place so far away that the closer they got, the further away it would seem to them.

You can see them in that vision, exhausted, stressed, ill and sick. They paid too high a price for their incessant quest for something they could not define, something so abstract like success, recognition or prosperity.

It occurs to you that if the price for those things is too high, perhaps if the goal is wrong, perhaps those people were looking for something that they could have achieved but in a more enjoyable way.

It dawns on you that the real goal is to delight in the path you are on. The river in the future might be wider, it might be deeper, but it will still be the same river. It occurs to you that the plants and the birds will be similar, the sun the same, the bench as soft. But where you are is where those things are, to try to obtain something different by pushing yourself to the point of exhaustion is a pointless exercise.

Enjoy your current path, and then when you are ready, move on at your own pace. The measure of your success lays in the present time, the things that you are doing at this moment. Future gains can be illusory if you ignore the pleasure in your quest for them.

You see a bird overhead, its wings flapping as it gains height, and then it stops and glides for a while before flapping again. The bird will get to where it wants, but with enough energy left to do what it has to do. As your eyes follow the flight of that bird, you see that your destination is very close by, a short cut across a beautiful meadow full of bright yellow and red flowers.

A short cut that would have evaded you had you kept on going intent on following the path. A short cut that did evade those people you saw in your images in the river, those people who were too busy rushing along the path to see where they were going in the longer term.

You stroll lazily across the field, feeling the sun smiling on you, smelling the scent of the flowers, feeling the grasses as they caress your legs. You are content. You are arriving at where you want to be.

SHAPE SHIFTING

Take a deep breath into your stomach. Bring to mind a picture of a castle turret from an old tale. Stand in that turret and look over the edge and see a little wooded area with a dirt track leading out. And on that track there are two men on horseback. The man in front has a big bird on his arm.

Sitting on a black horse, the first man is wearing a dark brown leather tunic. The second man is riding a brown horse and is wearing a bottle green tunic.

They look up at you and wave a greeting. You acknowledge them and turn to the top of the spiral staircase. Slowly you walk down the stone stairs until you reach the door at the bottom.

You walk across the courtyard, past two guards at the main gate. They bow their heads as you walk out to cross the wooden drawbridge.

You stroll to the two horsemen, and as you look back along the track you can see the Wise Man riding out on his huge white mount. He nods and smiles at you. He is a friend as well as being a healer and wizard.

His huge bushy white beard contrasts with the blue robe that is speckled with stars and moons. Little white flakes of bread in his beard make it seem as if stars are also shining from his face.

He rides up to you slowly, dismounts and hands his reins to the second horseman. He bows and says that he is ready to take you on a journey to the place for guidance, healing and reconciliation.

He points to a little stone wall behind you that is the height of a footstool. He asks you to climb onto it and then squat in the position of a bird just about to take off.

You do this.

He explains that soon he will say a word to you that will transform you into a bird and you will then fly upwards into the sky.

He speaks a word that is any word you want as your magical spell and you feel yourself soaring into the air.

(Note. If you forget your word in the future, just invent a new one. There is no pressure to remember it.)

Look down and see the castle turret, the other buildings and the two horsemen and the three horses below you.

You have the sharp eyes of a bird of prey and you can see little animals scurrying around. Rabbits, moles and voles. Other birds fly around, seemingly undisturbed by your presence.

You become aware of the landscape. To your right the small wood extends to meadows that make a patchwork towards a low cliff that hovers over a white beach that leads out to a calm and beautiful blue ocean.

In front of you there is a high mountain with snow on its peak.

Half way up, or half way down, you can see a huge waterfall gushing water into the valley below with foam and spray. Above the waterfall there is a huge double rainbow arching into the sky.

To your left a forest extends to the horizon.

Where the right edge of the forest meets the left foothills of the mountain there is a circle of sandy soil.

Beyond that part, the landscape turns into savannah.

Fly to that circle of sandy earth. You are aware that another bird is flying alongside you, and you know that it is the Wise Man. He is showing you these places, this landscape. It is the world that has always existed in your mind and imagination.

In the sand there is a smaller circle of low stones that are soft to sit on about the size of settees. In the middle of those stones you can see an old tree that, at some point in its history, had been struck by lightning. It is like a grey ghost that stands, watching its world.

At its base you can see a rock that is the size of a small column, a little pillar, half the height of a man. On it you can see an object that you quickly forget, consciously, but will always remember unconsciously.
You sit on one of the soft stones and relax. You explore the surroundings with your eyes. There are caves in the foothills where you can remember your past, recognise your present life and visualise your happy future. Get up and explore them if you wish,

now or in your next visits.

At this moment we will play a little.

Think of a wild animal that you admire. It can be big or small. If it lives in the Savannah, walk to the part of the circle that leads there. If it lives in a wood or forest, walk to the part of the circle that leads there. If it lives in meadowland, walk to that edge. If it lives in the hills or mountains go to the part of the circle where the rocks are.

Squat down, once again, but this time in the pose of the animal you admire. Say the word you heard that turned you into the bird and feel yourself transform.

Look down and see you new feet. If you are furry, see the fur, if not, then see your new skin.

Move into your chosen habitat and explore. See other animals. Smell the scents and perfumes of this new, temporary world. Run around, jump if you can. Stay there for as long as you like. Introduce others of the same species into this place. Let them symbolise your friends and family. Let them represent people you have yet to meet if you are lonely.

A major factor is that this place is totally harmless. There are no poisons, no fangs, no claws that hurt. The energy for life in this place comes only from love and warmth.

When you have enjoyed being this new animal in this new environment, say the word to yourself again and turn into a huge, beautiful eagle. Slowly flap you huge wings and fly towards the sea. The mountain should be on your left. Cross the meadows and then the beach.

Fly over the water and then dive softly, head first into the waves. As you break through, be aware that you are now a dolphin.

Swim and swim. Feel your back propel you through the sea. Then look at the bright corals and the fish that seem to reflect their blues, oranges, greens and reds. Swim faster and now accelerate to the surface, breaking into the air, making a somersault and splashing back in.

Continue swimming and playing with other dolphins.

Continue to dream of health and happiness. Chatter away to all the life that you can see.

Then, when you are ready, swim to the surface and leap into the air. Become the first bird that you became and fly back towards the castle.

When you get there, settle on the low stone wall and turn back into yourself. Step off the wall, thank the Wise Man and the two horsemen, return through the gateway, climb the turret stairs and stand in the place where you started.

This is the way to get to the place where you can be any creature that you would like to be.

And there is more!

To get there quickly, then just think of the item on the stone pillar in the circle of sand and you are back in the heart of this place. If you want you can change that.

Perhaps a chalice of health, maybe an object that means something special to you. Possibly something that you eat to give you confidence

POSTSCRIPT

A LECTURE FROM A MODERN SHAMAN

This is a long account of the thoughts of a modern shaman, an old man who had built businesses that would profit others rather than himself. He was an Indian by birth, but had grown up in the West.

I met him during a thunderstorm whilst on holiday with my family and the following is his view of modern life and its correspondence to the lives of our ancestors. With his permission, I tape recorded what he said and he agreed that his words could be included in this book.

Some of his words have inspired a few of the stories and metaphors in this book. His other words are given to you to consume as we eat fish. Avoid the sharp bones and enjoy the sweet meat as you wish.

"Religion is a business. It is a corporation. You find that the higher up the corporate ladder the employees go, the less spiritual they seem to become.

Knowledge is power and the more knowledge that people have that others lack, then the more power can be wielded. Secret knowledge is part of ritual. Ritual is what stops ordinary folk from being able to be spiritual. Their religions impose rules that have to be obeyed in order to appreciate life after they have died. I have always been intrigued by the modern Hollywood image of witchcraft. Like prayers and responses, spells need to be learnt and they must be delivered in special, esoteric ways.

It is a strange thing that the supernatural entities only seem to hear in Latin yet the demons haunt, hate and curse in the everyday language of their victims."

The lightning flashed again as the old man spoke. I shuddered when the thunder detonated above. It was like there was an something angry listening.

"You see. If the scene is set correctly, more power is added. If I had been a religious man searching for the souls of other men, I would have studied the weather and delivered my proclamations against a backdrop of a day like today. Wind and rain, hail and loud noises. I would have predicted eclipses and sold them as signs from the Heavens. Yet, the seers of old knew the weather patterns. Power was, and is, knowledge. And power is the lifeblood of the corporation."

My attention was fixed on the old man's words. I was hungry for more. "So, when you say the holy men look for the souls of others, what do you mean?" I asked. He slowly stated to answer my question.

"The corporations, whether the church, business or governments only want to sell the brand. The individual has no room in a company. The individual is the person who has a soul. The soul is not the thing that devils want to steal but it is a belief in life and happiness and the world on which we live. If we care too much for those things then we might protest against the felling of rain forests to make flat-pack furniture. We might buy smaller cars that use less gasoline. We might feel happy with the land we have rather than using force to invade other countries. We might just become the human that we feel inside but seem impelled to deny. We work for money rather than food. Money is the symbol of power. I want you to recover your soul. Your soul is part of the God of Spirituality. The God image used by religion is the thing that takes away the souls of men. They are mortgaged for the promise of a reward after our bodies and minds have worn out in the production of wealth for corporations."

The old man continued after he drank a glass of water.

"Did God create man in his own image or did man create God as a man who lives in the sky to ensure that we looked up in our spiritual moments to avoid looking at the real creation, our planet? Was it to prevent us from seeing God in ourselves and every living thing? God is not a man. God is the essence and the energy of all things above, below and around us. We are connected, as every point of a spider's web was at some point connected, to the builder's body. And everything is still connected to the whole.

"Shamans and the older witches knew that. That is why they have been eradicated or subdued. Their truth conflicts with the man made imagery of a super-power. That creation of God in a man's image stops us looking at the magnificent planet on which we live. While men are looking for God in the sky, their eyes are diverted from seeing the theft from, and the raping of, the organ and spirit of our creation, our Mother Earth.

"We are individuals in our primeval roots. We are also pack animals that will follow leaders for safety, order and security. When we became big societies we had to be controlled by the powers of force by using soldiers. The leaders became monsters instead of alpha males. They had the strength of force to murder others. They could invent mating ceremonials in order to rape. It is said that big is beautiful. Big is ugly.

Small is better. With small, the leaders are able to be challenged. They are accountable. Corporations are beyond reach. You have no say in the tax rates levied on you. You have no influence over the prices pharmaceutical companies charge for their drugs.

"Above all, you lack the right to refuse. The President is not chosen by the American people, he is chosen by fellow politicians and businessmen. The voters only vote for one man. The same applies to the Prime Minister of Britain. There is no choice, only an apparition of democracy. And if either of them does things that upsets the population, like starting wars, how the hell do you get rid of them? You can't."

I was now listening and processing at a pace. I nodded for the old man to carry on.

"By the way, the word Parliament comes from the root word that means 'speaking'. Where is the part in the mother of democracy that refers to 'listening'? And the very word 'corporation' comes from the Latin root for a body made of flesh. Souls are emotional. When souls are claimed then it is easier to get people to sacrifice their flesh in wars. The promise is that when the body is lost, the soul is saved and lives on. That pledge of immortality goes to the heart of emotional blackmail.

"I run a benevolent company. One that gives far more than it takes. My corporate goal is to ease suffering by protecting the innocent at the expense of the guilty.
I remember in a village in India, the people would chase the monkeys away in case they tried to steal food. One day I saw a monkey with a broken arm wandering down the road. I asked why it had not been killed or chased away. I was told that as it was unable to look after itself, then it became the responsibility of the villagers to care for it. In that simple way, a whole new philosophy of life emerged for me."

The storm was moving on leaving just rain rather than thunder and lightning in its wake..

The old man, a shaman who, ironically, ran a corporation, continued. "The celebrity cult reflects the need to feel good about ourselves by association with others who have done better. We love to build actors, pop-stars and television presenters only to glory in their falls. We make them gods and watch as they plummet like falling angels onto the rocks that smash them.

"As a child I had been intimidated by the power and seeming eternity of the sea. The waves were powerful and could wreak so much destruction when they were angry. They must have travelled the whole ocean in search of a cliff or beach to die on. They had so much pent-up energy that could be spent as a caress on a swimmer or as total destruction in a tidal wave.

"The aborigines of Australia, the native Indians of North and South America. The tribes of Africa and the Siberians and Eskimos. Those varying cultures are all tied together by the same approach to healing, an approach that is at the heart of psychotherapy. They are the principles that were adopted by Carl Gustav Jung. And at the centre of their beliefs is the idea that the world is a living thing. The concept is that the planet is alive with energy and spirits. Their relationship with Mother Earth is a symbiotic one where each party helps the other.

"Our twenty first century approach of so-called civilised people is purely parasitic. Men extract the life from the Earth, they cut down rain-forests, pollute the oceans, and drain oil to burn with nothing given in return apart from negatives. Global warming comes from laziness and greed. Cars, factories and so on.

"We live a nightmare. We are balanced between the new masters and the old slaves. People working every hour to build luxury items for the Western markets at low cost. People are used like machines in factories that have no safety rules. They use toxic chemicals that strip life away from workers who get nothing in return. Animals are killed to extinction for their skins. Forests are stripped to make furniture. Drug barons sell humiliating deaths for money. People are murdered for profit, and I include tobacco companies in that group of thugs.

"Most people seem to use the spiritual path for their own benefit. I have wondered about monks who sit and pray for hours in order to achieve their own peace with God. The modern preachers are pseudo-healers. They sell concepts of ritual to folk who want to find peace. They teach that we should look outwards to find God and inwards to find our faults. They need to turn the idea on its head. God, the Universe is within us and the problems are outside in the world. By caring for the world and its suffering we come to terms with our inner conflicts by default. Instead, priests make us frightened of retribution.

"Pseudo-shamans take our money for spells. The real shamans were, and are, healers of people, animals, plants and the planet. They gave their souls to save others. They took the risks of travelling into the world of evil spirits that, today, would be the psychoses of psychotics, to help alleviate suffering. They never did it for material gain. It was never the way it is now. Civilisation takes from the life of the world for short term gain. We need to experience the world rather than possess its assets. Rather than having, we need to be. We make ourselves miserable by striving to have more than we need. As a result of personal greed we are killing our planet; we are strangling our mother, the Earth.

The old man paused for a long while and he started again. "What I love most about my body is its perfection.

"The systems work beautifully without me having to think about anything. My heart pumps, I breathe, I digest, my temperature is controlled better than the average air-conditioning units and my hormones are measured and balanced without me having to lift a finger. And I could go on and on. I think that I am a perfect self-regulating capsule of flesh, nerves, bone and blood.

"We would be very boring if we were all robots like the Stepford Wives. And as my body looks after itself, then I have the time to do the more enjoyable things in life such as eating, drinking and loving. Some of our bodily activities, like breathing, are semi-automatic. Others such as temperature control may be assisted by wrapping ourselves in warm clothes or throwing ourselves into a pool, river or ocean. We sometimes feel like passengers in those life-supporting bodies. We relish the external world through its smells, tastes, sights, sounds and feel. That is why I am perfect. And so are you. Your body works in the same way as mine."

I was a little bewildered by the lack of modesty this man seemed to have. He continued.

"However, for every yin, there is a yang. For every minus there is a plus. Many years ago, what I hated most about my body was the excess fat that put my blood pressure up and threatened my good life by clogging my arteries. What disturbed me was that sense of panic and stress that seemed to run my life. As life-forms, we demand balance. As people we hope for relief from our problems.

"In the beginning we were a species that wanted to live. We needed to survive in order to avoid the pains of death. Most of all, we wanted to enjoy the pleasures of mating and, consequently, rearing the next generation.

"However, our world was full of creatures that saw us as nothing more than a herd of animals that tasted good and were easy to catch. Some creatures found us to be a threat and developed venom. We had to learn how to avoid the snakes and spiders in a rapid way. One mistake and we were dead. In this, nature was a great ally. It provided us with exquisite tools for survival. Life was simple and sensuous even if short because we lacked medicines in a beautiful, but deadly, Eden.

"In our modern and comfortable worlds we still have those tools that kept us alive for hundreds of thousands of years, those internal systems, senses and emotions over which we assume we have little control. They are beyond our conscious bidding. They can cause us to panic. We can develop fears and sometimes we feel unable to control our bowels.

"Somehow we feel driven to store more fat than we need. And, as those systems seem to be unrestrained we feel incapable of having any influence on them.

"Anxiety and corpulence behave like delinquents. It is true that direct intervention is unable to help, but we are able to persuade, coerce and trick our bodies and minds into doing what we want. We are able to survive our survival systems.

"When people describe others as primitive, what do they mean by this insult? We are, apparently biologically identical to our ancestors from tens of thousands of years ago. Rather than being primitive we are a species that has acquired a thin veneer of so-called civilisation. We use that to over-value ourselves against other animals and human societies. The dawn of mankind as a modern creature was when a human made a tool for killing something. And so civilisation continued to develop.

Language and social communication are perhaps not the preserve of humans. Listen to birdsong or wolves howling. The hiss of a snake says, "leave me alone, or else", and this is from a creature that is deaf!

"Perhaps the need to manufacture weapons came from our fundamental weakness and our powerful drive to survive. After all, we were born devoid of horns, claws, fangs, scaly armour and fur. This left us weak and vulnerable. Even the best Olympic sprinter could not outrun a lion. A heavyweight boxing champion could not put a fully grown gorilla onto the canvass. However, our weapons gave us a chance. A knife became a claw, a spear, an antler. We became able to strip fur from our quarry and wear it to keep us warm. Humans became able to change the world to their own design rather than having to adapt to the environment.

"And so our survival systems started to become redundant. We had systems that had kept us on this planet way before we developed weapons. We knew how to run away from danger. We knew how to forage. We knew how to hide. We were able to store fat to give us reserves of energy when times were hard. We had borrowed body hair to keep us warm.'

"Hair grew long on the head to increase our appearance of size and importance. Now, somewhat paradoxically, men shave their faces and trim their locks while women shave their legs and underarm hair. Why? Women are encouraged to paint their faces to resemble the sexual signalling of our cave ancestors. Breasts are lifted to make them look more milk productive and thus better for a prospective mate who wants to breed.

"All of this is done in the name of fashion. All of this is to make us look different to our ancestors. Ironically, we use colognes, deodorants and perfumes to substitute for our pheromones. This makes us all like our, so-called primitive, ancestors! Modern life has striven to modify facets of our nature. We are in denial of our primordial natures even though war is part of our historical and present lives. We hear news of rapes, murders, thefts and wars every day. We think we have control, but there is something deeper than our conscious-thinking that still runs us. They are the primeval killers that stalk us.

"The shamans and their cultures should be the guardians of the Earth. And what is happening? Now I have seen, at first hand, how the aborigines and North American Indians have been corralled into settlements. Their credibility has been erased by the application of alcohol, something for which they have very little tolerance. It is an effective but savage to gain submission and control.

"Other cultures watch their habitats, the rain-forests and savannahs, being chain-sawed to the ground to provide furniture for the rich countries or stripped to grow crops for the Western consumers. Even India is being invaded by the all-pervasive need to become high-tech. The old beliefs will disappear. What we can surmise is that the true faiths are being buried by the new Trinity of Money, Luxury and Selfishness.

"There is a God, and that God is the essence of the Earth. God created the world and then man created God in his own image in order to usurp the very essence of God, the creator of beauty and balance. The mistake, or strategy, is that we have given God a human form, and that form includes our failings. God is the planet, the universe, life and creation. We have personified God as a superhuman. We need to learn that God is the spirit of life, beyond blame, beyond judgement.

"The Ten Commandments, the basis of Judeo-Christian culture, are the words that exhort us to live the line, but which break their own credo by the implicit threat of damnation to those who do not adhere to them. Sin is thereby defined as our true nature. Thereby deliverance is our acceptance of the nature of man within the organised crimes of civilised countries such as war and social divides.

"A nation can covet its neighbour's ass and commit murder, rape and steal during its invasion, mostly in the name of God. Sadly, God lets it happen and nobody pays a price. Instead of pretending that we are a modern species born with innate social grace, we should recognise that we still have old people living inside us who live in huts and caves. We should deal with our behavioural foes as our ancestors did. There are no special rituals, unless we want them."

The storm was now over and the man left. I never saw him again but I kept the recording and my promise to include them here.

Other publications by the author include:

BOOKS

The Secret Language of Hypnotherapy
ISBN: 978-0-9550736-2-5

Short Stories and Metaphors.
ISBN: 978-0-9550736-3-2

SHORT STORIES AND METAPHORS AS AUDIO DOWNLOADS

Animal Nature
Metaphors that relax and change the way you think based on animal stories.

Human Nature
Metaphors that relax and change the way you think based on stories about people.

Nature's Nature
Metaphors that relax and change the way you think based on stories from nature.

Insight to Anger
Metaphorical stories about the destructive nature of anger and how anger can be overcome.

AUDIO FOR RELAXATION:

Fantasies and Dreams
Relaxation and positive thinking.

Self-Hypnosis
How to relax, visualise and set positive suggestions for yourself.

AUDIO FOR HELP:

Stop Smoking
How to stop smoking easily and safely using hypnosis and breathing techniques.

Weight Control
How to reshape your body using hypnosis and visualisation. This method has helped thousands of people.

More information from:
http://www.emp3books.com

Lightning Source UK Ltd.
Milton Keynes UK
UKOW03f2318081014

239843UK00001B/42/P